Country Roads of
FLORIDA

Country Roads of

FLORIDA

Drives, Day Trips, and Weekend Excursions

Second Edition

Bill McMillon

COUNTRY ROADS PRESS

NTC/Contemporary Publishing Group

Library of Congress Cataloging-in-Publication Data

McMillon, Bill.
    Country roads of Florida / Bill McMillon — 2nd ed.
      p.   cm. — (Country roads)
    Includes index.
    ISBN 1-56626-009-4
    1. Florida—Tours.   2. Automobile travel—Florida—Guidebooks.
    3. Rural roads—Florida—Guidebooks.   I. Title.   II. Series.
    F309.3.M39   1999
    917.5904'63—dc21   98-46277
                                              CIP

Cover and interior design by Nick Panos
Cover illustration copyright © Todd L. W. Doney
Interior site illustrations and map copyright © Leslie Faust
Interior spot illustrations copyright © Barbara Kelley
Picture research by Elizabeth Broadrup Lieberman

Published by Country Roads Press
A division of NTC/Contemporary Publishing Group, Inc.
4255 West Touhy Avenue, Lincolnwood (Chicago), Illinois 60646-1975 U.S.A.
Copyright © 1999, 1994 by Bill McMillon
Printed in the United States of America
International Standard Book Number: 1-56626-009-4
99 00 01 02 03 04 ML 19 18 17 16 15 14 13 12 11 10 9 8 7 6 5 4 3 2 1

Other titles in the Country Roads series include:

Country Roads of Indiana
Country Roads of Massachusetts
Country Roads of Michigan
Country Roads of Minnesota
Country Roads of New Hampshire
Country Roads of New Jersey
Country Roads of Ohio
Country Roads of Pennsylvania

Florida Country Roads
(Figures correspond with chapter numbers.)

Contents

Introduction

Introduction to the Second Edition

It was with great pleasure that I returned to Florida to revise this guide. I never tire of driving along the backroads of the state and exploring both familiar and new sites. Although it had only been a few years since I drove the roads included in the first edition, there were some noticeable changes in the towns along several routes. Sebring has been undergoing a building boom that threatens to change its quiet, almost sleepy tempo to a pace as frantic as the Orlando area's farther north, and the beach communities of the Panhandle have been changed by the tremendous hurricane forces that swept through the region in the intervening years.

None of this makes the back roads of the state any less attractive, however, and even the most experienced tourists can find new and unusual spots to explore in this delightful state. One word of warning—bed-and-breakfasts, small hotels, and restaurants have a high turnover rate, so those you read of here may or may not be in operation when you visit.

Introduction to the First Edition

This book was a travel writer's dream. I couldn't pass up an offer to select country roads of Florida and write about one- and two-day trips along them, and this guide is the result.

I traveled through a Florida that was far different, though not always far in distance, from the heavily visited, glitzy communities along both coasts; I chose lightly traveled roads representative of the state's diversity. I saw outstanding natural sites along some routes, visited important historical sites along others, and explored sections of Florida that few visitors, or even Florida residents, ever see.

The roads are arranged in a general north-south order in the guide, but I made no effort to place them in any special historical order or to arrange them in an order of travel. Nevertheless, the first route includes settlements made by the first Europeans in Florida, and the towns along the last have been strongly influenced by the most recent immigrants to the state.

After exploring the human and natural history of Florida, I better understand this complex state, whose theme parks and developed coastal regions are stereotypically modern American, yet whose isolated rural communities, often nestled amid large tracts of almost undisturbed wilderness, maintain a close identification with their southern heritage. This identification is best characterized by the numerous courthouse-square statues that commemorate the fallen soldiers of the Confederate States of America.

To simplify road designations, I've used the following abbreviations: I = Interstate; U.S. = U.S. Route or Highway; FL = State Route or Highway; County = County Route or Road.

1

Daytona Beach to
St. Augustine

Getting there: Begin in Daytona Beach. Follow FL A1A north to St. Augustine.

Highlights: The Casements, Tomoka State Park, Gamble Rogers Memorial State Recreation Area, Washington Oaks State Gardens, Marineland, Fort Matanzas National Monument, Bridge of the Lions, St. Augustine Lighthouse Museum, Castillo de San Marcos.

The site of one of the first European settlements in the nation in 1565, the east coast of Florida was the first area of the state to attract large numbers of northern tourists in the late 1800s and early 1900s. Heading north along FL A1A from Daytona Beach, you quickly enter Ormond Beach, where you can visit Tomoka State Park and The Casements, a 1912 cottage that was once the winter home of John D. Rockefeller. Beyond Ormond Beach you pass Gamble Rogers Memorial State Recreation Area; Washington Oaks State Gardens; and Marineland, built in 1938 as the world's first oceanarium, before reaching Fort Matanzas National Monument just south of St. Augustine. In St. Augustine you can see the Bridge of the Lions, St. Augustine Lighthouse Museum, Castillo de San Marcos, and old St. Augustine itself.

This is a one- or two-day round-trip of approximately 110 miles.

Once a lonely road that passed by long, empty stretches of coastal dunes along the Atlantic Coast and crossed deserted barrier islands off the east coast of Florida, FL A1A today leads through one of the most intensely developed regions of America. Along most stretches of shoreline, as well as on the many barrier islands just offshore, high-rise condominiums and luxurious homes block both views of and access to the oceanfront. One stretch of FL A1A, however, gives a glimpse at what the region was like before John D. Rockefeller and his associate Henry Flagler made the region from Jacksonville to Key West a refuge from the rigorous winters of the Northeast. This stretch lies between Ormond Beach and St. Augustine. Along here lies intermittent access to the ocean and the large tracts of land that have been preserved as parks.

A number of important Florida historical sites are within easy reach of FL A1A, and the first I visited was in Ormond Beach, just north of Daytona Beach. Both Daytona Beach and Ormond Beach were developed in the early 1900s as towns where tourists escaping from the frigid Northeast could spend at least part of the colder months, and many wealthy families such as the Rockefellers began to winter in the area regularly.

Henry Flagler, determined to develop the area as a "Southern Newport" winter resort for the wealthy, built a railroad and several hotels along the east coast of Florida, from Jacksonville to Key West. Though these accommodations attracted both the wealthy and the nonwealthy to the region, many of the truly wealthy, however, continued to winter in the Daytona area. John D. Rockefeller stayed at Flagler's majestic Ormond Hotel, a large wooden structure that was only recently torn down, until he reportedly became upset when he discovered that he was being charged more than other guests for the same accommodations. Rather than pay what he considered an exorbitant rate, Rockefeller in 1918 bought The Casements, an unassuming cottage on an eight-acre estate along the banks of the Halifax River.

Today the cottage at 25 Riverside Drive in Ormond Beach is home to the Ormond Beach Cultural and Civic Center, where various Rockefeller memorabilia are on view. I found the Casements site a good introduction to the early history of the region, and the center has one of the largest Boy Scout exhibits in the nation. Tours of the mansion and two acres of gardens are given Monday through Friday between 10:00 A.M. and 2:30 P.M., and on Saturdays from 10:00 A.M. until noon.

After visiting The Casements, I crossed over the Halifax River on Granada Avenue (the Birthplace of Speed Museum is located at 160 Granada and is worth a visit if you are interested in the history of auto racing and speed trials) to North Beach Street and headed north about three miles to Tomoka State Park. There I visited an antebellum homesite that has long since returned to a natural state. Moss-draped oaks lined the roads of the park, and I walked along raised boardwalks to the interior of the low-lying swamps and marshes, which have a scattered cover of the dense growth of shrubs and trees typical of coastal "hammocks."

I backtracked to FL A1A and headed north to Gamble Rogers Memorial State Recreation Area, where the road runs between a long, undeveloped beach on one side and sand dunes covered with low-lying coastal shrubs on the other. I stopped at one of the many access sites along the way and took a stroll on the beach. Unfortunately, I was there in mid-October and signs of sea-turtle activity were long gone. During the early summer several species of sea turtles leave the ocean, where they have adapted to the buoyant waters, to struggle over the rough coquina-shell beach to an area far above the high-water mark where they lay their eggs in sandy mounds. If you are traveling this route during early summer, you may be lucky enough to see some of them coming ashore after dusk, or at least to spot the wide tracks left as they drag their heavy shells through the sand.

Across the highway from the beach, near the northern entrance to the park, lies a short nature trail that leads through sand dunes covered with coastal scrub. I found it an excellent introduction to the coastal ecology that I saw during the rest of the trip.

About midway between Daytona Beach and St. Augustine, I stopped to explore one of the best-kept secrets of Florida's eastern coast. Washington Oaks State Gardens extends from the Atlantic Ocean to the Matanzas River and includes 390 acres of almost undisturbed coastal scenery. This small park includes a great number of plant communities typical of those found along Florida's eastern coast.

Between the highway and the park's beach are dunes covered with the coastal scrub that is the preferred habitat of the endangered Florida scrub jay. Along the beach you'll find one of the largest outcroppings of coquina rock in Florida. This rock, a natural composite of shells and sand, was used to build forts and other large buildings along the Florida coast during the Spanish occupation. The walls of both Fort Matanzas and Castillo de San Marcos were built of it, as were many of the early buildings in old St. Augustine.

Moving west, the scrub gives way to coastal hammock, and towering live oaks, hickories, and magnolias form a heavy canopy in which raccoons, opossums, pileated woodpeckers, and brightly colored cardinals thrive.

Along the Matanzas River, the hammock in turn gives way to tidal marshes, and you can see large numbers of wading birds hunting for small marine animals. Evening is a memorable experience, bringing subtle changes in the light as well as abundant insects. The setting sun is a perfect back-drop for the active birds that rise singly and in groups above the marshes, as though part of a staged choreography, then settle gracefully at more fertile feeding sites. As I watched their silhouetted dance, I strolled along the half-mile of nature trail that follows the edge of the tidal marsh.

Many people overlook the natural communities of the park as they concentrate on its human elements. No one inter-rupted my solitude as I explored the marsh, but I joined sev-eral people on a walk through the formal gardens and groves of carefully tended trees that are the remnants of the Belle Vista Plantation. Originally owned by Joseph Hernandez, a militia general during the Second Seminole War, the park was named after a distant relative of President George Wash-ington, a surveyor also named George who married one of Hernandez's daughters in 1844.

I continued north on FL A1A, and 40 miles north of Day-tona Beach came to Marineland, built in 1938 as the world's first underwater motion picture studio. A new word—oceanarium—was coined to describe this project. While the many newer oceanariums in Florida and around the country far outshine Marineland as tourist attractions, none can match the historic ambience of this slightly shabby park.

The park was an overnight sensation when it opened along this then-uninhabited section of beach, and it thrived until becoming a troop training arena and shark-repellent research center during World War II. After it reopened in 1946, an animal trainer from Ringling Brothers Circus was hired to begin experiments with training dolphins. These ani-mals were such a success that a special stadium was built to display the talents of a two-year-old dolphin named Flippy. And that was the beginning of today's large sea parks.

While I could have taken a whole day touring the two sections of this park, including a building that houses one of the largest seashell collections in the world, I wanted to move along to the important historical sites awaiting me. The first was Fort Matanzas National Monument, located some five miles north of Marineland and about 15 miles south of St. Augustine on the southern end of Anastasia Island.

From the late 16th through the early 18th century, Florida was a battleground where England, France, and Spain fought for religious and political dominance. From about the time St. Augustine was founded by Pedro Menéndez de Avilés of Spain in 1565 until the English took control of Florida by treaty in 1763, there were almost constant skirmishes along the coast near St. Augustine.

One such battle occurred between the French and Spanish in September and October 1565 and led to two massacres that killed a total of 300 French soldiers. The Spanish word for slaughters is *matanzas,* and the slaughters of the French Huguenot troops occurred near the present-day Matanzas Inlet, where the Matanzas River enters the Atlantic.

Over the next two centuries, the Spanish maintained a wooden watchtower and thatched hut on Rattlesnake Island, in the middle of the Matanzas River, near the inlet. From there a runner or a man in a log canoe could set out to warn St. Augustine if an enemy ship was sighted.

After an unsuccessful siege in 1740 by General James Oglethorpe, the founder of the first English colony in Georgia, the Spanish decided to build a more imposing fortification on Rattlesnake Island. Using coquina quarried on Anastasia Island (near St. Augustine), craftsmen from St. Augustine constructed a stone watchtower that housed five cannons and about 10 men. From the time the tower was completed in 1742 until the United States acquired Florida in 1821, the tower protected this approach to St. Augustine.

The fort and surrounding area are now a national monument; you can learn about the area's history at the visitors center and then take the park's ferry across the inlet to visit the fort ruins on Rattlesnake Island.

Continuing north along FL A1A, I passed a number of condominiums and apartment-like complexes between the road and the ocean that were often hidden behind a thick growth of vegetation. Ignoring the first few Beach Access signs I passed, it was only when I decided to follow the directions of one such sign that I discovered the beach along here. The east coast of Florida is one of the few places in the nation with hard-packed sand capable of supporting cars, and I soon realized that I could drive my vehicle along the beach where others had parked theirs while they took a stroll or picnicked. I took advantage of this opportunity and had a leisurely drive along the beach for a mile or so before returning to FL A1A.

The candy-striped tower of the St. Augustine Lighthouse stood high above the surrounding land to the north and drew me onward toward St. Augustine, but just before reaching it I discovered the 1,035-acre Anastasia State Recreation Area. There I found good beaches, abundant bird life, fishing, excellent swimming, and plenty of Windsurfers. As I was exploring the four major plant communities (sand dune, salt marsh, coastal scrub, and coastal hammock) in the park, I ran across the site of the quarry where the coquina used to build both Fort Matanzas and Castillo de San Marcos, as well as many other buildings in St. Augustine, was mined.

Between mid-June and late August the park also features a production of Florida's state play, *Cross and Sword*. This two-hour production has a cast of more than 50 actors, musicians, and dancers, and describes in depth the story of King Philip II and the early explorations of Florida by Captain Pedro Menéndez and his crew. Don't expect political correctness in this play, but enjoy it for the period piece it is.

As I left the Anastasia State Recreation Area, I was again drawn to the St. Augustine Lighthouse standing 165 feet above sea level and marking the entrance to St. Augustine Inlet. The present lighthouse, completed in 1874, was the last in a series of lighthouses constructed by the Spanish, English, and Americans between 1690 and 1874 to send out beacons of light to sailors. The light still operates, although the light-keeper no longer lives in the two-story Victorian coquina-and-brick house that sits at the base of the tower.

I stopped and browsed through the coastal museum of lighthouse and local history exhibits, now housed in the restored lightkeeper's home, which was almost totally destroyed by fire in 1970. The Junior Service League of St. Augustine began an eight-year campaign to restore the building in 1980, and it opened to the public in 1988.

I also watched the half-hour movie, shown several times each day, that tells the story of those who have kept the light shining in the tower for more than 100 years. I passed on the climb to the top of the tower, however, since I wanted to get to St. Augustine before it was too late in the day. The light-house and keeper's house are at 81 Lighthouse Avenue, Anastasia Island.

As I returned to FL A1A from the lighthouse, I noticed the St. Augustine Alligator Farm across the highway. This century-old research center, one of the original tourist sites along the coast below St. Augustine, houses the oldest collection of alligators maintained in a controlled environment. I didn't stop in here since I have seen many alligators in the wilds of Florida, but you may want to take a look at these primitive creatures in captivity.

From the lighthouse it is only a short drive north to the Bridge of the Lions, a picturesque old structure that links Anastasia Island with old St. Augustine as it spans the

Matanzas River and Intercoastal Waterway. And St. Augustine is the end point of this trip.

St. Augustine, the oldest continuously occupied European settlement in the New World, is the city that ensured Spain's control of Florida for several centuries. Today the city is a mecca for historically inclined tourists from all over the nation. From the oldest wooden schoolhouse in the country to the oldest store, St. Augustine provides visitors with many buildings that span the history of European settlement in the United States.

More than 400 years old, the city today features narrow streets, sweeping beaches, grand homes, and the oldest fort in the country, Castillo de San Marcos. All of these give St. Augustine more sightseeing spots than any other city in Florida.

The best taste of old St. Augustine can be found along St. George Street, just south of the old city gate, where many of the restored buildings house shops and museums in which you can shop until you drop. (Cars are restricted in this area.) There are plenty of other sites outside of the St. George Street area, though, and the best way to get an overview of them is to take one of the trams or horse-drawn carriages. St. Augustine Historical Tours at 167 San Marco Avenue takes tourists on a seven-mile, 16-stop educational tour of St. Augustine. These tours, which begin at the old jail, can also be boarded at any of the 15 other stops.

Carriage tours such as those offered by the Gamsey Carriage Company provide more private and personal tours of the city. Starting at the Bayfront, you can take a one-hour tour during the day or a 45-minute tour in the evening.

For those who don't want a tour, the best way to see the city is to put on good walking shoes, park anywhere on the perimeter of the old section near the city gate, and walk until there is nothing else to explore. And this can take a while.

Castillo de San Marcos

Among the sites that you don't want to miss, whether you take a guided tour or explore on your own, is the Castillo de San Marcos. This large and impressive fort, built between 1672 and 1695, has never been conquered by invading forces—although it has been occupied by Spanish, British, and U.S. forces at various times in its history. The imposing structure cost King Philip almost $30 million, but the residents of St. Augustine were never bothered by pirates after it was completed. Its impregnability was due to the thick coquina stone walls, which absorbed the blow of cannonballs without crumbling. Though its use is now limited to being a national monument, the fort has been in constant use for more than 300 years.

If you choose to explore St. Augustine on your own (which I did; this is the best way to find all the picturesque spots in the old city), begin with a stop at the St. Augustine Visitor Information Center at 166 San Marcos Avenue, just north of the old city gates. There I picked up plenty of brochures that told me about what to see and do while I was in St. Augustine. Be sure to ask there about showings of *Dream of Empire* and *Struggle to Survive,* two films about early life in St. Augustine. Again, don't expect these films to portray the early Europeans as rascals who destroyed the way of life enjoyed by the indigenous peoples. Instead, enjoy them as period pieces that were made to depict the Europeans in as favorable a light as possible.

You can spend the night in one of the 16 bed-and-breakfasts that are members of the Historic Inns of St. Augustine if you find your day too short to see all the sights along the route and still have time to thoroughly explore St. Augustine. Then spend another morning exploring the city before returning to your starting point. You can write to the association at P.O. Box 5268, St. Augustine 32084 for a complete listing of members.

If you spend a night in St. Augustine and have your choice of when you can do so, try to make it during the Spanish Night Watch Weekend. Soldiers from the Castillo reenact a battle, crafts are sold in the old city (and many of the craftspeople demonstrate their skills), and musicians, dressed in 18th-century attire, stroll through the town playing for all to hear. Nonparticipants join the celebration by leading a candlelight processional through the city.

Although FL A1A is far from being a true country road, it provides a good introduction to the origins of Florida, preparing travelers for the strong Spanish colonial influence that still permeates much of the state.

For More Information

The Casements (Ormond Beach): 904-676-3216

Birthplace of Speed Museum (Ormond Beach): 904-676-3346

Tomoka State Park (Ormond Beach): 904-676-4050

Gamble Rogers Memorial State Recreation Area (Flagler Beach): 904-517-2082

Washington Oaks State Gardens (Palm Coast): 904-446-6780

Marineland of Florida (Marineland): 904-471-1111

Fort Matanzas National Monument (administered by the National Park Service at Castillo de San Marcos) (Summer Haven): 904-471-0116

Anastasia State Recreation Area (St. Augustine): 904-461-2033

St. Augustine Lighthouse Museum (St. Augustine): 904-829-0745

St. Augustine Alligator Farm (St. Augustine): 904-824-3337

St. Augustine Historical Tours (St. Augustine): 904-829-3800 or 800-397-4071

Gamsey Carriage Company (St. Augustine): 904-829-2391

Castillo de San Marcos (St. Augustine): 904-829-6506

2

Lake City Loop

Getting there: From Gainesville, follow I-75 north about 30 miles to the beginning of this trip. This route follows U.S. 90 from Lake City to Sanderson, and then FL 229 north to the Osceola National Forest, before returning to Lake City on FL 250.

Highlights: Columbia County Historical Museum, Olustee Battlefield State Historic Site, Ocean Pond, Florida National Scenic Trail, Big Gum Swamp Wilderness, Osceola National Forest.

Stop at the Columbia County Historical Museum in Lake City before heading out on this trip. There you will learn much about the early years of the region.

The first stop past Lake City is the Olustee Battlefield State Historic Site. After visiting there you can explore around the Ocean Pond Recreation Area of the Osceola National Forest or hike along the Florida National Scenic Trail.

Stop and explore the Big Gum Swamp Wilderness on your return trip.

This is a half-day, 60-mile loop.

Lake City has been a transportation hub since early Native Americans passed through the region as they traveled from the Okefenokee Swamp to settlements in central Florida. Today it sits at the intersection of I-10 and I-75, where both trucks and tourists speed by. Those who stop in Lake City find a farming community that caters to outlying Columbia County farms large and small and that grow trees, watermelons, soybeans, corn, tobacco, and peanuts.

Rather than focus on its Spanish heritage, as does St. Augustine, Columbia County focuses on its southern heritage and has several attractions that commemorate the Civil War period. To gain more information about this era when Florida seceded from the Union, I visited the Columbia County Historical Museum in Lake City.

The museum is housed in a building from about 1870, of southern Italianate style with a typical square shape and low-pitched roof. John Vinzant, Jr., the first clerk of the court of Columbia County and a disabled Confederate veteran, purchased the house in 1880, and his daughter, May Vinzant Perkins, lived there until she died at age 92. Ms. Perkins was a respected poet and writer who was named poet laureate of the state of Florida prior to her death; many of her writings are on exhibit at the museum.

Although the building was erected after the Civil War, many of its most popular exhibits feature artifacts and memorabilia from the war. This didn't surprise me, since I had already observed the local sympathies for this long-lost cause. As a native southerner, I was well aware of how strongly most of the Deep South still identifies with the Confederacy, but was somewhat surprised at the depth of this feeling in the Florida Panhandle.

After visiting the Columbia County Historical Museum, I know how strongly these feeling still run through the community, though, and this was more than reinforced as I drove 15 miles farther along U.S. 90 to the small crossroads community of Olustee.

This drive took me through country that was far from the wealthy and prosperous farming communities I was to see later in the upper Panhandle, or even those close by Lake City, so I was not surprised to find little more than a few rundown homes and a dilapidated store and gas station where FL 231 crosses U.S. 90 in Olustee. The community springs to life every February, however, as Civil War buffs converge on it to participate in the second largest Civil War reenactment in the country (the largest is at Gettysburg). This reenactment is held at the Olustee Battlefield State Historic Site, about two and a half miles east of town. This park is the site of the largest battle to take place in Florida during the Civil War.

On February 20, 1864, twelve regiments of Union soldiers (5,500 men) with 16 cannons engaged about 5,000 Confederate troops at Olustee. Unfortunately for the Union troops, who had left Jacksonville earlier in the month, they ran into a planned defense position where the southern troops could easily defeat them.

From midafternoon until dark a battle raged between the two forces on the floor of the pine forest, which was free of undergrowth. At dark the Union troops, realizing they could not defeat the Confederate soldiers, began a hasty retreat. In that short time the Union forces suffered 1,861 casualties, whereas the Confederate soldiers suffered 946.

This battle has retained its importance to the residents of the area as a matter of regional pride; as early as 1899 the Florida legislature created a commission to select a site and raise funds to build a monument commemorating the battle. The monument was completed in 1912 and dedicated in 1913, just 49 years after the battle.

Today more than 1,200 men from across the United States, equipped with weapons used in that long-ago war, faithfully reenact the events and movements of that historic engagement each February. And for residents of the Florida Panhandle, it is still a "we versus they" battle. A friend of mine in California recalls the first time she visited the battle-field. As the docent talked about how "They had their troops over there" and "we had our troops here," she felt obliged to ask who the "we" and the "they" were. Though the answer would not have been surprising to any native southerner, it did surprise her when the docent said, "Why, 'we' is the South, and 'they' is the North." Regional feelings obviously still run high here.

One of the natural obstacles that impeded the movement of the Union troops during the battle was Ocean Pond, a large natural lake of 1,760 acres. The lake is now a camping and day-use area operated by the Osceola National Forest, and the Florida National Scenic Trail runs nearby. You can reach it by returning to FL 231 and driving north for about a mile, or you can take the scenic trail from the trailhead at the bat-tlefield for about two miles. There are 23 miles of the trail in the Osceola National Forest, and 20 plus boardwalks offer a dry view of the swamps and wetlands that are found throughout the flat woods of the area. I explored along the boardwalk between the battlefield and Ocean Pond before continuing on U.S. 90 to the small community of Sanderson. The short hike led me through the wetlands that surround the open pine forests of the battlefield, and I could see how the Union troops had been led into an ambush in an area where they had little room to maneuver.

A bit larger than Olustee, Sanderson shares that town's involvement in the Civil War fighting and is no more pros-perous. Its houses all have the worn-out look of homes far past their prime, barely resisting the insistent forces of nature.

I took a left on FL 229 in Sanderson, and drove through

what would have been called the "colored" section of town in my youth. Although much progress has been made in addressing the civil rights of minorities in Florida, and we are much more politically aware of what we say, many small towns in the South have changed little in either attitudes or actions in the past 50 years. And one legacy of the Old South in these small communities is the very definite dividing line between the black and white sections of town.

A colorful part of black life in the rural south is the small "juke" joints that can be seen along many back roads. One of these, complete with full-face drawings of black performers on its outside walls, sits just north of U.S. 90 on FL 229. I didn't stop for this one, for I have visited many such joints over the years, but you may want to stop by one on your travels. Expect puzzled expressions that seem to say "Are you lost or something?" as you walk in, but after the initial shock you will be welcomed freely by the owners and clientele.

FL 229 quickly leaves the outskirts of Sanderson and takes you deep into the thick pine plantations of the Osceola National Forest. There I felt far removed from the congested coastal regions of Florida and even from the open farmlands that I had just driven through. These thick stands of pine form a canopy that, keeping the sun from reaching the forest floor, darkens the mind and soul of all who enter the forests. On even the brightest day there is a gloom that pervades the land, and this is reflected in the small, depressed communities scattered throughout the region.

FL 229 joined FL 250 just a few miles south of the southern end of the great Okefenokee Swamp, which drops down into northern Florida from its vast reaches in Georgia. While the roads do not reach deeply into the swamps, I skirted the edge of one as I took a left on FL 250 to head back toward Lake City.

FL 250 runs beside the Big Gum Swamp Wilderness, a part of the Osceola National Forest. This large, nearly level, freshwater flat has a relatively undisturbed cypress-gum swamp in the center that is surrounded by pine flat woods. The groundwater table is always near the surface in the area, and many times reaches more than three feet above it. This makes exploration of the area tricky. A thick, spongy mat of decayed and growing organic material covers much of the ground's surface, and it is difficult to tell when you are going to sink through to standing water and when you can safely cross an opening.

I explored a little of the swamp, however, by parking in a designated area about one mile past the junction of FL 250 and FL 235. There I walked a short distance along the remains of an old tram bed that rises above the water level. In dry times you can make a three-mile loop on this bed and explore about a mile into the swamp before you return to FL 250 near the FL 235 junction.

Although much of the timber in this area was logged extensively between 1915 and 1920, nearly all the intrusions made by the logging have now been covered by the luxuriant growth of the swamp. Today Big Gum Swamp is almost back to its natural state, and is very similar to what it was like during the 1500s when Hernando de Soto led his expedition along the De Soto Trail, which U.S. 90 closely follows.

After stopping at Big Gum Swamp, I returned to Lake City on FL 250.

For More Information

Columbia County Historical Museum (Lake City):
   904-755-9096 or 904-752-2485

Olustee Battlefield State Historic Site (Olustee):
904-752-3866

Florida National Scenic Trail (Olustee):
904-752-2577 or 904-378-8823

Big Gum Swamp Wilderness (Olustee): 904-752-2577

Osceola National Forest (Olustee): 904-752-2577

3

Monticello to White Springs

Getting there: From Tallahassee, take I-10 east to U.S. 19, and U.S. 19 north to Monticello, a 25-mile trip. The route, which begins in Monticello, follows U.S. 90 east through Madison, the Suwannee River State Park, and Live Oak. It then turns onto FL 136 and continues east to White Springs. The return trip follows FL 136 and I-10 back to Tallahassee.

Highlights: Monticello County Courthouse, Perkins Opera House, Madison town square, Suwannee River State Park, Dixie Grill, Stephen Foster State Folk Culture Center.

Monticello is famous for its historic area, where large Victorian and Greek Revival homes are among the 40 buildings from the 19th century that give you a peek into a time when cotton was king in Jefferson County. Also worth visiting are the acoustically perfect opera house, which has been restored to its original opulence, and the courthouse, which was patterned after Thomas Jefferson's home in Virginia.

In Madison you can see more 19th-century buildings, as well as a town square with monuments commemorating both fallen Confederate soldiers and Colin Kelly, a Madison native and the first Medal of Honor winner in World War II.

After Madison, stop at the Suwannee River State Park before continuing on to White Springs and the Stephen Foster State Folk Culture Center.

This full-day trip is 80 miles one-way.

If I had to pick one trip that best characterized the panhandle region of Florida, this might be the one. Jefferson County is known as the Keystone County since it is the only one in Florida that extends from Georgia in the north to the Gulf of Mexico in the south. The county seat and only incorporated town, Monticello (pronounced Mon-ti-SELL-o by natives), is a living reminder of the pre–Civil War period when cotton was king and living was easy (at least for those who owned the land and had the money). And the area even has its Spanish connection: U.S. 90 follows the old Hernando de Soto Trail. There are historical markers along the highway that explain the trek de Soto made with 600 soldiers and assorted livestock along old Native American trails in 1539. This route along U.S. 90 passes through country that's among the wealthiest farming regions of the Panhandle, and certainly more prosperous than most rural farming areas in the state. The Suwannee River, long an important river in Florida and southern Georgia, runs along the eastern edge of this region. The area was one of the earliest and most prosperous cotton-growing regions in Florida, and its citizens were among the most outspoken proponents of secession prior to the Civil War. They rang bells, built bonfires, and held parties when Florida seceded from the Union. To this day the Old South is still much in evidence, and still celebrated, in the region.

I began the trip in Monticello, where I met with several surprises. Nothing had prepared me for the magnificently preserved historic district, which is largely intact from the 19th century, and the towering Avenue of Oaks that was planted in 1889 on one of the main approaches to town.

The buildings here are of Greek and Classic Revival designs and give one a true feeling of the Old South. Even the commercial buildings are worth a look. Among all of these wonderful structures, however, one built at a cost of only $40,000 is the centerpiece of the town. This is the county courthouse, patterned after Thomas Jefferson's home. This small building with a silver dome is an eye-catcher, and easily the most photographed building in town, but the restored Perkins Opera House, built in 1890, is probably the most visited.

Monticello became the cultural center of north Florida after the 600-seat opera house, with the largest stage in the Southeast, was completed. By the 1930s, though, the building had been converted to a movie theater, and even that folded in the latter years of the Great Depression. In the 1960s the Perkins was scheduled for demolition to make room for a modern gas station on the site. The local residents, who had already begun to restore many of the old buildings in the historic district, rescued the opera house, however, and restoration began in the early 1970s. It was completed in time to celebrate the building's centennial in 1990.

The Chamber of Commerce (420 Washington Street) publishes a walking-tour map of the historic district that includes information about many of the homes and commercial buildings, as well as about the Jefferson County Watermelon Festival (with its renowned watermelon seed–spitting contest) that is held each June. Those who would like to spend the night in Monticello and begin a trip the next morning will find several restored homes that serve as bed-and-breakfasts.

From Monticello I headed toward Madison, 32 miles away on U.S. 90. This section of the route leads through rural farmland with many groves of hardwood trees, such as maple, oak, and dogwood, that change from green to vibrant reds and yellows in the fall, when U.S. 90 becomes one of the few "fall color tours" in the state.

There are still a number of plantations between Monticello and Madison, including one owned by media magnate and Atlanta Braves owner Ted Turner. Both the plantations and the smaller farms raise watermelons, pecans, peanuts, and cotton as cash crops. More than one-third of all the pecan trees in the United States grow here, and they add to the fall colors.

I was still in rolling hills as I reached the small community of Madison, a typical Deep South town. In the middle of the business district I found the silver-domed county courthouse and its adjacent park, complete with its Confederate monument. The courthouse was completely renovated in 1988, and the courtroom was restored to its early appearance.

The Madison town square also has several other monuments, as well as a bandstand where bands often play on warm summer evenings. One monument is dedicated to Colin Kelly, a Madison native who was the first U.S. Medal of Honor winner in World War II, and to the four freedoms mentioned by President Franklin Delano Roosevelt in his annual State of the Union message to Congress in January 1941. The four freedoms are freedom of speech and expression, freedom of worship, freedom from want, and freedom from fear everywhere in the world. The 1914 courthouse is far from the oldest building in town, as the small wooden Episcopal Church was built in 1843 and the oldest house in town (which is still occupied) was built in 1849.

Although Madison's historic homes do not match Monticello's in either number or majesty, they are still worthy of a driving tour, beginning with the centerpiece Wardlaw-Smith house. This 1860 Greek Revival mansion, which sits across the town square from the courthouse, was being turned into a bed-and-breakfast when I visited. That is a long way from its stint as a Confederate hospital after the Battle of Olustee (see Chapter 2).

The First Baptist Church is also worth visiting. Although it seems to be a fairly typical church building from the outside, when you enter you unexpectedly find an octagonal worship area.

There are many large oaks in Florida, but the one behind the Wardlaw-Smith house is huge even by Florida standards. Since it was planted in 1830, the tree has grown to more than 80 feet in height and almost 20 feet in diameter; it has a spread of almost 150 feet.

Tobacco is the largest crop grown in Madison County today, but it was cotton that brought refugees from South Carolina to the region in the early 1800s. Here they grew some of the finest long-staple cotton in the world, and before the boll weevil wiped out cotton as a cash crop in Florida in 1916, the largest cotton-processing plant in the world was located in Madison. Sixty-five gins were driven by a 500-horsepower engine. The 16-foot drive wheel for that engine still stands near the railroad; you can see it as you enter town from the south. In most years a small patch of cotton grows near the drive wheel to remind the citizens of Madison of their heritage.

Beyond Madison U.S. 90 leaves the rolling hills as it approaches the Suwannee River. Not quite 20 miles from Madison I came to the river and the entrance to the Suwannee River State Park, an excellent rest stop. The park sits at the confluence of the Withlacoochee (the one that begins in Georgia, not the one located farther south in Florida) and the Suwannee rivers near where a railroad bridge has crossed the Suwannee since before the Civil War. In fact, the Union troops that were defeated at the Battle of Olustee (see Chapter 2) were headed here to destroy the bridge and cut off supplies to Confederate troops in southern Georgia. The remains of the earthworks that the Confederate soldiers constructed to defend the bridge are still evident near the ranger station.

I overstayed my intended time at the park because there were several interesting trails that I couldn't pass up. The first was the Sandhills Trail, which took me from the picnic area near the park entrance to the old Columbus Cemetery. Prior to and during the Civil War, Columbus was a bustling town that stood near the railroad crossing, a ferry, and a large sawmill. Little remains of that community except its cemetery.

After the short hike to the cemetery, I returned to the picnic area and walked along the river to see the remains of the Confederate earthworks as well as the ferry landing. As I stood along the river at the ferry landing, I had no trouble visualizing a steamboat coming up the Suwannee to the Withlacoochee—as such vessels frequently did more than a century ago.

The rivers were running low when I was there, and it was easy to see evidence of springs bubbling from the banks of both. The Swannacoochee Springs along the banks of the Withlacoochee are the largest of these, but even they are small compared to other springs I saw later in my travels. I worked my way upstream alongside the Suwannee, past the picnic area and boat ramp to the footbridge that crosses the Lime Sink Run. On the other side was the Suwannee River Trail, which follows the river upstream before winding through the dense growth of a hardwood hammock to the banks of the Lime Sink Run.

Lime Sink Run is a spring-fed stream that flows through limestone outcrops on its way to the Suwannee River. On my way along its banks I saw signs of beavers, but no beavers themselves, although I was later told that quiet visitors frequently see them at dawn and dusk.

I wanted to stay longer at this park, and wished that I had a canoe to head upriver on the Suwannee River Canoe Trail (which begins in Georgia and ends in the park), but time was running short and I still had to reach the end of the trip: White Springs and the Stephen Foster State Folk Culture Center.

The Suwannee River begins its 250-mile journey to the Gulf of Mexico in the southern reaches of the Okefenokee Swamp in southeastern Georgia. This meandering river had long served as a major transportation route for the region, with steamboats slowly moving up and down the river filled with passengers and cargo, when Stephen Foster made it famous throughout the nation with his song "Old Folks at Home." Today its circuitous path leads it around three sides of Suwannee County, just below the Georgia border.

The area between the Suwannee River State Park and Live Oak, the county seat of Suwannee County, is the center of the tobacco-growing region of northern Florida. Even with all the adverse publicity about smoking, tobacco is still a major crop in several states, and it accounts for about one-third of farm employment in Suwannee County.

Other major agricultural enterprises in the Live Oak environs include poultry production, dairy farms, and watermelon growing. More than 650,000 chickens are processed every week in the Gold Kist poultry plant that I passed between the park and Live Oak. That's more than one million drumsticks!

Continuing on U.S. 90, I stopped for lunch in Live Oak, a prosperous farm community with few tourist attractions or amenities, and discovered the Dixie Grill on the corner of Howard Street and Dowling Avenue. The menu there boasted, "It's not Suwannee River country without catfish," and that's what I ate: large pieces stacked high on a plate with plenty of cole slaw and hush puppies piled around the edges. Nothing fancy; just good southern cooking.

The biggest event in Live Oak each year is the Christmas on the Suwannee Festival, which is held the first weekend in

December. More than 10,000 people converge on Live Oak for the arts and crafts show, entertainment on the courthouse square, and a Christmas parade at night. The Suwannee County Fair, the oldest in Florida, is also held in Live Oak each October.

From Live Oak I took FL 136 to White Springs, a lovely little town that sits on a sweeping curve of the Suwannee River and is the home of the Stephen Foster State Folk Culture Center. White Springs has long been a gathering place, and the Native Americans in the region regarded the springs as a sacred site. They are even said to have declared a five-mile radius around the springs as a safety zone where injured braves could recuperate from their wounds without fear of being attacked.

The region became refuge for another group during the Civil War, as plantation owners from South Carolina brought their families to the isolated site during the heaviest fighting. Many of these families stayed after the war was over, and helped reestablish cotton as a major crop in the region.

By the end of the 19th century, White Springs had become a fashionable spa that attracted many well-known people, including Teddy Roosevelt. Today the concrete structure that was built around the springs in that earlier period still stands, but it is no longer used.

The primary attraction in the community today is the Stephen Foster State Folk Culture Center, and I enjoyed the varied activities offered there. Foster never lived in Florida, and never saw the Suwannee River, but he is nevertheless intimately connected with the history of the Suwannee region. "Old Folks at Home" was designated as the official state song in 1935, and the Folk Culture Center revolves around Foster's music.

In addition to a large exhibit of Foster artifacts, however, the museum has outstanding educational exhibits relating to a number of Florida's ethnic groups. The Crackers, Conchs, Cubans, African Americans, and Seminoles are all represented in exhibits with dioramas that depict their contributions to Florida's history.

As I walked around the well-kept grounds and along a trail near the river, I heard the carillon tower peal out beloved Foster melodies every half hour. I was particularly impressed with the arts and crafts center, where I bought several articles made by local craftspeople. Although I didn't take one, guided tours of the carillon and visitors center are available, as well as boat tours on the Suwannee River. All of these seemed to be popular.

In addition to the permanent attractions, there are several special events sponsored by the Florida Folklife Program of the office of the secretary of state every year. These include an old-fashioned Fourth of July celebration and the Florida Folk Festival. It's well worth organizing a trip around the latter. Generally held the middle two weekends in November, during the traditional end of harvest time in Florida, the festival provides visitors a peek at Florida life during earlier periods. Demonstrations of traditional crafts and skills are scheduled continuously during the two weekends, music is played, and many items and food are available for sale. The festival is very popular with local schools and residents, and that makes it a special occasion during which you can meet many locals as they explore Florida's past.

If you would like to spend the night in White Springs before making the return trip, you might try one of the bed-and-breakfasts that open sporadically in town. These are generally in large, older homes that have the ambience of a life long since gone in most towns, and they are furnished with antiques that complete the feel of a time when White Springs drew wealthy tourists with time on their hands.

At the end of your trip, take FL 136 back to I-10 and return to Tallahassee on I-10.

For More Information

Monticello Historic District (Monticello): 850-997-5552

Perkins Opera House (Monticello): 850-997-4242

Jefferson County Watermelon Festival (Monticello):
  850-997-5552

Suwannee River State Park (Live Oak): 850-362-2746

Dixie Grill (Live Oak): 850-364-2810

Suwannee County Fair (Live Oak): 850-362-7366

Stephen Foster State Folk Culture Center (White Springs):
  850-397-2733

4

Tallahassee to Apalachicola

Getting there: From Tallahassee, this trip follows FL 363 south through Woodville and the Edward Ball Wakulla Springs State Park to U.S. 98. It follows U.S. 98 through Panacea and Carrabelle to Apalachicola. The route for the return trip is north on U.S. 98 to U.S. 319, then north on U.S. 319 to Tallahassee.

Highlights: Natural Bridge State Historic Site, Wakulla Springs State Park, St. Marks National Wildlife Refuge, San Marcos de Apalache State Historic Site, Posey's, Gulf Specimen Marine Laboratories Aquarium, St. George Island State Park, Apalachicola National Estuarine Research Reserve.

The Natural Bridge State Historic Site and Wakulla Springs State Park are the first two stops on this trip. St. Marks National Wildlife Refuge and the San Marcos de Apalache State Historic Site are near St. Marks, a small fishing village on Apalachee Bay. Also in St. Marks is Posey's, home of the "topless oyster."

Between St. Marks and St. George Island, you can visit the Gulf Specimen Marine Laboratories Aquarium, eat at another Posey's restaurant, and walk along Carrabelle Beach. On St. George Island you can visit the St. George Island State Park and St. George Inn before heading into Apalachicola.

This is a two-day, 170-mile round-trip.

In Florida's early years few people had any inclination to venture into the vast wilderness areas of the state's middle and southern regions. The two most important cities in Florida then were St. Augustine and Pensacola, each representing significantly different regions and neither wanting the other to become the capital of the new state. The disputing political factions compromised. They would build a new city halfway between St. Augustine and Pensacola, and they would make it the state capital.

From that compromise sprang Tallahassee, today a bustling governmental center and university town that sits among the rolling hills of the Florida Panhandle. To the north of the town are the rich farmlands that produce peanuts, watermelons, and tobacco; to the south are miles of swamps and pine forests that reach to the Gulf of Mexico, where some of the most productive fishing waters in the world are located.

After a short drive down FL 363 from Tallahassee, I came to Woodville, where signs directed me to the Natural Bridge State Historic Site about six miles to the east. During the final weeks of the Civil War a group of Confederate troops, along with many old men and boys from the Tallahassee area, thwarted an attempt by Union troops to capture Tallahassee in a five-day battle at this site on the St. Marks River.

The Confederates won this battle and drove the Union soldiers back toward St. Marks, but they lost the war, which ended within a month of the battle. Nevertheless, their victory kept the Union Army out of Tallahassee, and that city remained the only Confederate state capital east of the Mississippi River not to fall into Union hands at any time during the war.

I walked around the markers and remaining battleworks, and wondered once again at the intense involvement that many residents of the Old South maintain with that long-ago war. Each March the Battle of Natural Bridge is reenacted on the weekend nearest the anniversary of the actual battle (March 3–7). Authentic Confederate and Union encampments are set up, and realistic war action allows visitors to get a feel for how Civil War battles were fought.

Farther along FL 363 dense forests stood high along both sides of the highway. About 13 miles south of Tallahassee, I came to the Edward Ball Wakulla Springs State Park, a large wilderness park surrounding one of the largest and deepest freshwater springs in the world. Throughout Florida's panhandle and central sections, hundreds of such springs flow out of the vast underground caverns that riddle limestone formations beneath the surface.

These springs are natural wonders that often boggle the mind with their power. Wakulla Springs had a peak flow of almost 15,000 gallons per second on April 11, 1973, and water continues to flow from an unbelievably large and complex underground cavern at a rate of about 10,000 gallons per second. In 1958 divers explored the cavern beneath the 4.5-acre basin fed by the spring. They swam more than 1,000 feet into the cavern and more than 250 feet underground—at which point, they said, their bright lights revealed "an ever-deepening, ever-widening cavern." Fossils of extinct animals such as the mastodon have been discovered in the depths of the cavern, and archaeologists continue to make new discoveries in this and other springs throughout the state.

I spent some time exploring the natural wonders that can be seen on the land around the springs and then took the 30-minute glass-bottomed boat tour, on which I could see the entrance to the underwater cavern some 120 feet below the water's surface. The tour also leads through forests of ancient cypress trees with their "knees" rising above the waters and downstream to the Wakulla River (which begins with Wakulla Springs), home to abundant numbers of alligators, snowy egrets, herons, and ibis.

The springs and surrounding swamps and forests are so primitive and lush that they have been used by Hollywood as the site for several famous movies. The early *Tarzan* movies with Johnny Weissmuller were filmed here, as was the 1950s epic *The Creature from the Black Lagoon*.

I didn't stay or eat at the old lodge in the park, but it is worth a visit in itself. In fact, you might want to stay overnight there as the start of this trip. The lodge was built by billionaire financier and conservationist Edward Ball, who had married into the Du Pont family. Ball purchased the land around Wakulla Springs in the early 1930s and built a 27-room, Spanish-style lodge that opened in 1937. The lodge features Tennessee marble floors, ornate ceilings, antique furnishings, and magnificent, blue-heron fireplace andirons. Guest rooms are decorated individually with plenty of period pieces, but each has modern conveniences such as private baths and air-conditioning. The restaurant features southern-style cooking at moderate prices.

I reluctantly left Wakulla Springs to continue my trip, but could easily have spent the rest of the day exploring there. Other sights were awaiting, however, and I wanted to get to St. Marks National Wildlife Refuge before the heat of the day drove the wildlife to cover.

The trip continued along FL 363 through the Apalachicola National Forest until I reached Newport and U.S. 98. I took a left there for a short drive to the entrance of the St. Marks National Wildlife Refuge, one of the largest and oldest wildlife refuges in the eastern United States. My first stop here was the visitors center, where I looked at the interpretive displays before venturing out into the refuge.

The 95,000-acre refuge, established in 1931, includes large tracts of hardwood swamps, pine flat woods, pine-oak uplands, saltwater marsh, and open water in Apalachee Bay. The area is famous for the large number of alligators that live there as well as for the many migrating birds that pass through. Mid-November through December is the best time to see migrating waterfowl (the refuge is the only wintering area in Florida for Canada geese); shorebirds are most common in late spring and early fall. The bird list for the refuge includes 272 species of birds that are considered to be part of the local fauna; mammals—including white-tailed deer, raccoons, skunks, foxes, and bobcats—are also frequently sighted.

From the visitors center I took the six-mile scenic drive through the refuge to the 150-year-old St. Marks Lighthouse, one of the oldest in the Southeast. The 80-foot tower was built in 1831 from stones removed from the ruins of Fort San Marcos de Apalache, and its light continues to guide modern ships with the same lens it used during the Civil War.

With more time I would have hiked along some of the more than 30 miles of primitive trails that crisscross the refuge, but on that day I had to be satisfied with sighting several bald eagles, dozens of shorebirds and waterfowl, both large and small alligators, and a herd of white-tailed deer—all of which I saw on the drive from the visitors center to the lighthouse.

After leaving the wildlife refuge I returned to U.S. 98 and headed for the small fishing village of St. Marks. This village has obviously seen better economic times, and the number of boats that I saw from the road certified that fishing was the primary activity of the area.

I had planned on just passing through the town to see the museum and excavated ruins of Fort San Marcos de Apalache, but got sidetracked when I spotted Posey's. Although the building simply had the look of a waterfront bar, I couldn't pass by a sign that shouted "Home of the

Topless Oyster." The sweet-and-sour sauce that accompanied the raw oysters made the stop a good choice for lunch, and I continued on to the fort with a full stomach. The restaurant is open only during the peak oyster season, between September and April.

The fort at the San Marcos de Apalache State Historic Site was built in 1679 by the Spanish, but was also occupied by representatives of the British, the United States, and the Confederacy before falling into disuse. General Andrew Jackson captured the fort in 1818, and that was an important factor in the United States's acquisition of Florida in 1819. Today the museum has many artifacts from all the forces that have occupied the fort. You'll also find a good trail winding among the ruins and earthworks on the way to the point where the Wakulla River joins the St. Marks River. If you are lucky (I wasn't), you may catch a glimpse of the gentle giant of the seas, the manatee, from the river overlook at the end of the trail.

I returned to U.S. 98, and followed it west through the southern edge of the Apalachicola National Forest and the small town of Medart to Panacea, which sits on a small inlet off Ochlockonee Bay. There I spotted a sign near the IGA Shopping Center that directed me to the Gulf Specimen Marine Laboratories Aquarium. Located in a residential section of town, at the corner of Palm Street and Clark Drive, this small facility is the brainchild of internationally known researchers and authors Anne and Jack Rudloe.

A wide variety of marine life from the Gulf of Mexico is on display at the aquarium, and I handled sea squirts, starfish, and various seashells in several touch tanks. Inside the building marine biologists were packing live specimens for shipment to schools and other research centers.

I returned to U.S. 98 by way of Rock Landing Street and drove by another Posey's restaurant. This one is open year-round and is quite different from the run-down wooden building in St. Marks. The blue metal building has the appearance of a large warehouse and no outside ambience whatsoever, but I am told the food is just as good as in St. Marks.

After Panacea, U.S. 98 crossed Ochlockonee Bay and began to follow the shoreline closely. Unlike other coastal areas of Florida, this stretch has no high-rise condominiums and green golf courses, for tourism is not a major industry in this area. Fishing is, and the small villages along the highway are most definitely fishing villages, complete with the smell of day-old (or more) bait and heavily used tackle. I was thankful for the lack of tourist establishments as I drove and as I stopped at several deserted beaches. All the beaches along this section of the gulf shore have sand so dazzling white that it sparkles in midday sun. I made the drive in early October and received an extra special surprise as I walked along the beaches. Hundreds, if not thousands, of migrating butterflies of several species (mostly monarchs) fluttered from bush to bush along the edge of the beach and added splotches of brilliant color.

As I approached the small village of Carrabelle I saw a large island offshore, the first of several barrier islands that protect the shoreline from gulf storms. This was Dog Island, seven-and-a-half miles long and connected to the mainland only by ferry, which also serves a mail boat that makes the trip to the island three times a week. The Nature Conservancy owns about three-fourths of the island, and only about 100 homes are spread over the other quarter.

The closest thing to a commercial establishment on the island is the Pelican Inn, which has eight sparsely furnished apartments. Guests have to bring all their own food and drink when they rent the apartments, and there are no TVs or telephones. Entertainment is obviously limited. There is a hot tub at the inn, and there are miles of deserted beach for hiking, shell collecting, and bird watching. You can even walk among the highest sand dunes in Florida.

One recent guest volunteered that he and his wife had thoroughly enjoyed themselves during their stay. "There isn't anything that I can think of that could beat the night we took a stroll on the moonlit beach with the stars overhead and the waves lapping gently on the hard sand at our feet." You can take the ferry out to the island for the day for about $10 each way, but I had to continue on my way. There were other barrier islands for me to explore later in the day.

Dog Island isn't the only spot to visit in Carrabelle, however, and I didn't miss the world's smallest police station. It was hard not to, however, for it is a public phone booth along U.S. 98 with a large American flag painted on it. When the patrol car isn't out on a call, it's parked next to the phone booth, waiting for the next emergency.

The next 20 miles were relatively more developed than the drive between Panacea and Carrabelle. Compared with driving along either coast of the lower peninsula of Florida, the coast here seemed wondrously free of condos and motels. By Eastpoint there was more commercial development, however, and I almost missed the road to the 29-mile-long St. George Island.

I took the six-mile bridge and causeway, which had been a toll road until only recently, and stopped several times to watch the oyster boats working one of the largest oyster reefs in the world. I was amazed at the loads of oysters being hauled aboard by the oystermen and women using large tongs that looked heavy and unwieldy. I shouldn't have been surprised, though, for most of the oysters harvested in Florida come from the reefs in Apalachicola Bay.

St. George Island had more development than I had expected, but most of it is on the west end of the island. This

large barrier island is very narrow, never stretch-
ing more than a mile across. As I headed
toward the east end, where more than
1,800 acres have been protected within
park boundaries, building became less congested, although there were still many homes in the
middle of the island and along the gulf shore. The park
itself includes more than nine miles of white sand beaches
backed by high dunes covered with sea oats. In addition,
there are slash pine forests and acres of live oak hammocks.

The best places I found to see the limited wildlife of this
arid island were in the area of the marshes on the bay side.
There I spotted some diamondback terrapins, as well as several types of shorebirds. After a visit to the park I returned to
mid island, where I had earlier passed the historic St. George
Inn. This inn is the oldest lodging establishment on the island.
Each of the eight rooms has a water view, either of the bay
or of the gulf, and is furnished with a queen-size antique bed.
Although I did not stay over at the inn, it is an ideal stop for
those who are spending the night in the Apalachicola area
before returning to Tallahassee. If you plan to stay overnight
in Apalachicola itself but want to have lunch or dinner on the
island, the St. George Inn offers excellent food served in a
tasteful setting.

Many private homes here also offer accommodations for
one or more nights. The best place to find out about these is
at the Anchor Realty and Mortgage Company of St. George
Island, which handles many of the rentals on the island.

I returned across the causeway and continued on to Apalachicola across the Gorrie Bridge, which rises high above the
mouth of the Apalachicola River, the largest natural waterway in Florida. The city of Apalachicola, founded as a cus-
toms post at the mouth of the river in the early 1800s,
gradually grew into the third largest port in Florida as large

cotton plantations developed to the north. Use of the port dwindled after a Civil War blockade and the development of railroads in northern Florida.

At that point residents of the region turned to the sea and the forests for their employment, and Apalachicola experienced another boom period that lasted until the Depression years of the 1930s. Since then the city has remained a small town the tourist industry has largely ignored—but one well worth the traveler's time.

As I entered the downtown area from U.S. 98, the first building that caught my eye was the historic Gibson Inn. This large structure was built in 1907 of cypress and heart pine that had been personally selected by the builder, James Buck. The inn has been lovingly restored and is one of more than 50 restored buildings that are part of historic Apalachicola. Several of the old homes have been converted into bed-and-breakfasts with period furnishings.

I walked around the wonderful wide veranda that encircles the Gibson Inn before entering the refurbished lobby with its old-fashioned bar. I was drawn to the gracious dining room, where it was easy to slip back almost a century, eat at a civilized pace without pressure to give up my table, and experience Apalachicola as it was in times past.

At the inn I found a guide for walking and driving tours of the historic area; following it, I wandered past the old post office and customhouse, a large cotton warehouse, the sponge exchange, several Greek Revival homes, Trinity Episcopal Church, and the John Gorrie State Museum.

John Gorrie was a doctor in Apalachicola from 1833 until his death, and during one outbreak of yellow fever he developed a method for cooling his patients' rooms. This early ice-making machine was the beginning of modern refrigeration and air-conditioning, although Gorrie was unable to market his invention before he died in 1855.

There is much more to Apalachicola than the historic district, however, as a trip to the Harbor Master House at the city-owned marina in Battery Park proved. There the St. Vincent Wildlife Exhibition describes how the Apalachicola River and bay have long played an important role in the life of local residents.

Today, with fishing the primary industry in the region, both state and federal agencies recognize the importance of maintaining the quality of the fisheries in the bay. Together they have developed several preserves where the resources are managed and protected. All of Apalachicola Bay, from the western end of St. Vincent Island to the causeway between Eastpoint and St. George Island, is included in the Apalachicola Bay Aquatic Preserve, which is managed by the Florida Department of Natural Resources. The Apalachicola National Estuarine Research Reserve is a cooperative effort among Franklin County, the state of Florida, and the National Oceanic and Atmospheric Administration.

Staff members of the estuarine reserve lead tours of their facility near the marina, where the scientists study the ecology of the estuary at the mouth of the Apalachicola River. This area, where the tidewaters of the gulf mingle with the freshwater of the river, is rich in sea and marsh life. After a visit there, I investigated boat trips to St. Vincent Island National Wildlife Refuge, which is also part of the reserve. St. Vincent Island is a large barrier island that is unlike most barrier islands in that it is not long and narrow. More than four miles wide at points, it has almost 15 miles of beaches, and about eighty miles of sand roads that crisscross the island and lead by freshwater lakes and swamps.

This is an outstanding outing for adventurous sorts who like to watch for birds (more than 200 species have been seen on the island); search for signs of loggerhead turtles, which lay eggs on the beach; and find alligators basking in the sun.

I didn't have time to take a trip to the island, but promised myself that I would the next time I was in the area.

An easier way to view the river and bay is on M/V *Apalachicola Belle,* a 30-passenger flat-bottom riverboat with a shallow draft which is very similar to the riverboats that operated on the river in the late 1800s and early 1900s. The boat departs from the docks at the Boss Oyster Restaurant at 125 Water Street and offers several types of cruises on the river and bay.

Although I was a little early for it, preparations were already beginning for the oldest and largest seafood festival in the state. The Florida Seafood Festival is held the first weekend in November each year to honor Florida's largest seafood-producing area, Apalachicola Bay. Oysters, shrimp, crabs, and fish abound in the waters of the bay, with over 90 percent of the oysters and half of all the shellfish in the state coming from there. The festival offers visitors a chance to participate in tonging, oyster shucking, net casting, and crab races, as well as to taste some of the best seafood found anywhere. If you have a chance, take this trip at the time of the festival weekend.

Return to Tallahassee by U.S. 98 and 319.

For More Information

Natural Bridge Battlefield State Historic Site (Woodville):
　850-925-6216

Edward Ball Wakulla Springs State Park (Wakulla):
　850-922-3632

St. Marks National Wildlife Refuge (Newport): 850-925-6121

San Marcos de Apalache State Historic Site (St. Marks):
　850-922-6007

Posey's (St. Marks): 850-925-6172; (Panacea): 850-984-2753

Gulf Specimen Marine Laboratories Aquarium (Panacea):
850-984-5297

Pelican Inn (Dog Island): 850-697-4728 or 800-451-5294

St. George Island State Park (St. George Island): 850-927-2111

St. George Inn (St. George Island): 850-927-2903

Anchor Realty and Mortgage Company (St. George Island):
800-824-0416

Gibson Inn (Apalachicola): 850-653-2191

John Gorrie State Museum (Apalachicola): 850-653-9347

Apalachicola National Estuarine Research Reserve
(Apalachicola): 850-653-8063

Apalachicola Bay Chamber of Commerce (Apalachicola):
850-653-9419

5

Chipley to Ponce de Leon

Getting there: From Panama City, drive north on FL 77 for 45 miles to Chipley and the beginning of this trip. Turn onto U.S. 90 and drive east to Marianna, then north on FL 71 to Greenwood and Malone. In Malone, turn west on FL 2; continue through Campbellton and Graceville to FL 81. Turn south on FL 81 and continue to Prosperity and Ponce de Leon. To return to Panama City, follow FL 81 south, FL 20 east, and FL 79 south.

Highlights: Falling Waters State Recreation Area, Chipola River Seafood Company, Florida Caverns State Park, Great Oaks, Ponce de Leon State Recreation Area.

Just south of Chipley you'll find the only waterfall in the state of Florida, at Falling Waters State Recreation Area. From there, head east to Marianna, the center of a prosperous peanut-farming region. Florida Caverns State Park is just outside town. As you head north to Malone, don't miss the antebellum home of Great Oaks in Greenwood.

Jackson County produces more than 80 percent of the peanuts grown in Florida, and many of these are produced on the farms along FL 2 between Malone and Graceville. As you enter Graceville, look for the modern renditions of antebellum homes.

Enjoy the rolling hills and small cypress swamps between Graceville and FL 81, and when you see signs for local churches, take some side trips on the dirt roads that lead into the stands of pine on either side of the highway. Finish your trip at the Ponce de Leon State Recreation Area in Ponce de Leon.

This is an 80-mile one-way trip. Take either a half day or a full day.

Of all the routes in this guide, this one surprised me most. When I was looking at the map, I thought this drive would take me to country much like the poor hill country of such Deep South states as Alabama and Mississippi. I expected to see decrepit homes partially hidden among pine groves, and hardscrabble farms where elderly residents sat on front porches, rocking slowly in the summer heat.

Was I in for a shock! Jackson County, of which Marianna is the county seat, is one of the most prosperous counties in Florida. It produces more than half of the peanuts grown in Florida (the region is just south of the more famous peanut-producing area of Georgia), and is the number-one producer of soybeans in the state. With such productive croplands, the region is anything but poor. In place of the decaying homes scattered across unproductive land that I had anticipated, there are majestic modern homes that reflect their antebellum ancestry as they stand beside well-kept fields.

Although tourism is not an important economic factor along the route, the region contains more than farms and forests. I came to the first natural attraction just before I reached Chipley on FL 77. Signs led me to Falling Waters State Recreation Area, off FL 77A, three miles south of Chipley. There I saw the only waterfall in Florida. And a most unusual waterfall it was. As it percolates into the ground, rainwater, which

is a weak acid, slowly dissolves away the limestone under-
neath to create large caverns. These caverns are abundant
throughout the state. Occasionally the roof of one of these
caverns will collapse, leaving a large depression in the ground.
These depressions are usually funnel-shaped and have sloping
walls, but at Falling Waters Sink the collapse forms a steep,
smooth-walled chimney some 100 feet deep and 15 feet in
diameter. A small stream flows into this sink and forms a
scenic waterfall, one you view from above rather than from
below.

I watched the waterfall descend to the bottom of the sink,
where the remains of an early gristmill lie. Then I followed a
boardwalk to view other sinks, although none of them had a
waterfall. Afterward I walked along a trail that led through
the hardwood hammock surrounding the sink to a longleaf
pine forest. Both of these plant communities are maintained
by ecological burns that allow such wildflowers as Osceola's
plume and meadow beauty to flourish during the spring. The
trail also led me past the site of the first oil well ever drilled in
Florida. The well was not productive, and no other attempts
were made nearby.

From the park, bypassing Chipley, I followed U.S. 90 east
17 miles over rolling hills to the bustling farm community of
Marianna, incorporated in 1828. Today it flourishes without
the two things most areas of Florida depend on for economic
well-being—tourism and retirees.

As I drove through town I was struck by its prosperity. In
comparison to many of the towns I had visited farther east,
Marianna is a thriving community that is proud of its appearance. I found the Chamber of Commerce in the oldest restored
house in the county (built in 1848), and passed by many other
well-kept homes that were obviously built in the 19th century.
At the chamber I discovered that there are so many restored
homes in Marianna that the chamber publishes a "Historic

Sidewalk Tour" map. Although I found the tour less impressive than the ones in Apalachicola and Monticello, it did introduce me to the antebellum heritage of the community.

The major businesses face the town square, as they have since the town was built, and an obelisk in the square stands in memory of the "Cradle to the Grave" militia that defended the town against a Union attack in 1864. Since most able-bodied adult men had long since been conscripted into the Confederate forces, small boys and old men joined together to form the militia. More than 60 of them were killed or injured during the skirmish now known as the Battle of Marianna. The ironic part of this battle was that the residents of Marianna and surrounding areas had been noted for their staunchly pro-Union sentiments prior to the war and during its early years. These sentiments changed dramatically after the war ended, however, as the carpetbaggers began their rule of the region.

Today it is easy to engage locals in conversation about the battle and the people involved in it. I visited the St. Luke's Episcopal Church to see the pulpit Bible that had been saved during the battle and to find the tombstones of many witnesses to and participants in the skirmish. I didn't visit the battlefield site, but it is just east of town on U.S. 90.

I drove by two restored homes on West Lafayette Street that are now showrooms of fine antiques. The 1840 House, Ltd., and The Gallery occupy the buildings at 244 and 224 West Lafayette, and both rate a walk-through just to see the restoration work that has been done on them.

I had a good lunch at the Chipola River Seafood Company before heading north to the Florida Caverns State Park, some three miles out of town. On the way to the caverns new homes, showcases of the town's prosperity, line both sides of the highway near the country club. The caverns were created by the same geological action as the sinkhole at Falling Waters Sink, except the caverns were formed far enough beneath the earth's surface that their roof has not collapsed. Today the caverns are the only publicly accessible underground caves in Florida that don't require you to don scuba gear to explore them.

Although these caverns are certainly not in the class of other limestone caverns in the United States, such as Mammoth Cave in Kentucky, the stalactites and stalagmites that have formed in them over millennia are beautiful and well worth visiting. The park also has a disappearing river (the Chipola River runs underground there), a natural bridge, and the Blue Hole Springs (complete with a white sand beach).

After stopping by the caverns, I continued north along FL 71. This route led me through level to rolling farmland with large open fields and pastures. Beef cattle, horses, and hay farming appear to be the principal crops here.

About 10 miles north of Marianna is the small town of Greenwood, where Great Oaks, an antebellum home built in 1860, can be viewed from the highway. Although it is a private residence and not open to visitors, I stopped for a good outside look at this outstanding example of antebellum architecture.

After photographing the mansion, I continued on to the historic Pender's Store, where local farmers have been buying feed, seed, work clothes, and groceries from the Pender family for over a century. The store still had its old soda pop cooler and original 1869 heartpine floors and sturdy shelves when I dropped by. The talk around the place was all about how the crops had been that year and what kind of winter was coming.

After finishing my soda, I continued north through prosperous farm country to the small farming community of Malone, where I turned west on FL 2. Although not as affluent as Marianna, Malone is definitely not an impoverished area. Beef, peanuts, and pine plantations support plenty of productive farms in the region, and Malone is their commercial center.

Heading west from Malone, I entered some bottomland with hardwood forests and saw my first cotton about two miles out of town. These weren't the vast fields of cotton that I have seen in other cotton-producing areas of the South, but much more like the area where I grew up in northeast Mississippi. The largest fields of cotton here appear to be about 80 acres, and the accompanying homes look less prosperous than what I had seen around Marianna and Malone. I felt even more at home as I went farther west. The highway leaves the bottomlands and enters rolling land, and the signs leading to small country churches have many names I knew from my youth, such as Mount Zion and Friendship Baptist. The bottomlands with their thick growth of hardwoods alternate with rolling hills.

About 10 miles out of Malone I reached large tracts of pine-covered hills, more like what I had imagined this route would be. The homes in these hills are less prosperous looking (although there are no run-down tenant shacks, at least along the main road), and many narrow red-clay roads lead back into the pine forests. As in many other sections of the South, more activity takes place off the main paved roads than on them. These dirt roads often lead to small communities hidden from the outside world; many of these towns have been built around unassuming country churches.

I didn't follow my instinct to explore one of the dirt roads to see where it led, for I have visited hundreds of such small communities over the years, but I suggest that those who have spent little time in the South take one of them and follow it until it comes to a small community. Stop and buy a soda pop at the country store, which will probably be the only business in the area. There you will meet people who have little contact with the world at large, but who are always ready to share their lives and thoughts with you.

As you get closer to Campbellton, these side roads are more likely to lead to small black communities. In this section of Jackson County I had seen only African Americans, and any doubts I might have had about the makeup of the population were dispelled as I passed the Bus Stop Club, a juke joint with game room and bar. This building is typical of the Deep South, where blacks have given a distinctive character to their clubs. Brightly colored drawings on the outside walls let everyone know that a juke joint is inside. I passed through Campbellton without stopping, since the only building of any size was a farm supply and hardware store.

The land beyond Campbellton once again became higher, and the rolling farmland was obviously more prosperous than the previous 10 miles of bottomland and pine-covered hills. When I reached Graceville, there was no doubt left about its prosperity. As I entered this small town of about 2,000 residents, I passed about a dozen modern mansions of antebellum design. These were so impressive that I stopped at the first small grocery store and gas station to ask about them.

I really hadn't been prepared for the answer. According to the store customers and clerks, Graceville has one of the highest per capita incomes of any community in America, and the source of this wealth is peanuts. None of the homes is open for tours, but a casual drive around town to look at them is well worth the time spent. Other than the mansions there is little of great interest in Graceville, for it is really just another farming community, although a rich one.

I continued west on FL 2, passing a number of cypress swamps on farmland along the road. The first swamps are little more than small ponds with cypress snags and knees around the edge, but the larger ones farther on have a number of live cypress and other trees that are representative of cypress swamps across the South.

The 30 miles between Graceville and FL 81 pass through rolling farmland and small communities that are little more than crossroads. Esto, Miller Crossing, and Pittman appear on road maps, but the most you'll find in any of them is a gas station and a small grocery store. More often you'll see only a few scattered homes.

At FL 81 I turned south toward Prosperity, which shows little of that property. Then I continued on FL 81 to Ponce de Leon. The hills around here are some of the highest in Florida, which doesn't mean much. The highest spot in the state, a whopping 345 feet above sea level, is found outside the small crossroads of Lakewood, near the Alabama border off U.S. 331.

Just before FL 81 crossed under I-10, I came to the small town of Ponce de Leon. The legend of the fountain of youth has lived in Florida since the days of the explorer for whom the town is named. Although no one has determined which of Florida's many freshwater springs de Leon thought might be the fountain of youth, it probably was much like the springs located at the Ponce de Leon Springs State Recreation Area just south of town. Before I reached the recreation area, I passed a small furniture store where rustic furniture is made from willow branches. There are also several small antique shops in town.

The springs with their constant 68-degree temperature provide a refreshing respite from Florida's summer heat. Sitting in the middle of a 443-acre park, the springs and surrounding land have been used for all sorts of social gatherings since the 1920s. While the Smithgall family owned the spring, they built a wooden retaining wall around the main spring boil in 1926 to prevent erosion. In 1953, this wooden wall was replaced by a concrete wall, which has been maintained ever since.

The state park system acquired the property in 1970, and the site became a state recreation area where both residents and visitors can find relaxation and enjoyment. The main spring is fed by two large underground flows that produce more than 14 million gallons of crystal-clear water every day. The water's coming from deep within the limestone caverns is what maintains its temperature at a constant 68 degrees year-round, and visitors swim here most of the year.

I enjoyed the two nature trails, which provide great views of the 350-foot run from the main boil to nearby creeks and of the wildlife activity along the waterway. I thought the weather was a bit cool the October day I visited the park, but people were still swimming where the water gushes up into the spring boil, and none seemed the worse for it.

I ended my trip at the park, and returned to Panama City via FL 81, 20, and 79.

For More Information

Falling Waters State Recreation Area (Chipley): 850-638-6130

Jackson County Chamber of Commerce (Marianna): 850-482-8061

The 1840 House, Ltd., and The Gallery (Marianna): 850-482-5624

Chipola River Seafood Company (Marianna): 850-526-2837

Florida Caverns State Park (Marianna): 850-482-9598

Pender's Store (Greenwood): 850-594-3304

Ponce de Leon Springs State Recreation Area (Ponce de Leon): 850-836-4281

6

Gainesville to Cedar Key

Getting there: From Gainesville, take FL 24 southwest to U.S. 27A. Turn northwest on U.S. 27A and continue through Chiefland to FL 320. Turn west on FL 320 and continue to FL 345. Take FL 345 to FL 347; turn right on FL 347 and continue through Fowler Bluff to FL 24. Turn right on FL 24 and continue to Cedar Key. Return to Gainesville on FL 24 north.

Highlights: Florida Museum of Natural History, Manatee Springs State Park, Lower Suwannee National Wildlife Refuge, Cedar Key Scrub Preserve, Cedar Keys National Wildlife Refuge, Cedar Key Historical Society Museum.

Travel through open cattle-ranching and dairy country between Gainesville and Bronson. At Bronson take a side trip to visit the local park with a small spring. From there, continue to Chiefland and Manatee Springs State Park, where you will find a first-magnitude spring. Head south along the Suwannee River as the road borders the Lower Suwannee National Wildlife Refuge. In the refuge, stop at Shell Mound County Park before heading on into Cedar Key, the end point of this trip.

This trip is 80 miles one-way. It is a one-day trip, although many will want to take two days for it.

On my way out of Gainesville, often called the most livable town in Florida, I made a quick stop on FL 24 that could have taken my whole day. This was at the Florida Museum of Natural History—the largest natural history museum in the South and considered one of the 10 best museums of its kind in America—on the campus of the University of Florida. There I studied the displays of human and natural history in Florida that prepared me for the rest of the trip. If I had had more time, I would have made this a full day's outing and taken the drive to Cedar Key the next day; I would recommend this more leisurely approach to anyone who has the time.

After visiting the museum I headed southwest on FL 24, passed under I-75 about five miles out of Gainesville, and entered cattle-ranching, dairy, and hay-farming country. The road followed a straight line through this level region, passing the small communities of Arredondo and Archer before entering an area of pine plantations that shut off all views on both sides of the road. As the route took me closer to the gulf, it entered Levy County, which is home to 20 plus nature-based recreational sites. Because of this abundance of nature-related activities, Levy County is known as Florida's Nature Coast. Unlike other coastal regions of Florida, however, Levy County has no long white beaches along the gulf. Instead, there are river deltas and saltwater marshes where hundreds of wading birds can be seen among the reeds.

At Bronson, the first community I came to in Levy County, I stopped to look at a fascinating collection of birdhouses on the corner of FL 24 and U.S. 27A. No one was around to tell me about them, so I was content just to look before turning northwest toward Chiefland on U.S. 27A. About three miles out of town I noticed a sign to Blue Springs Park, and decided to find out what was there. I was somewhat disappointed after seeing some first- and second-magnitude springs in other parks, but found this small county park a good place to have a snack and stretch my legs a little. I didn't spend much time there, however, for I was headed to a much larger spring about 15 miles farther along.

I passed through Chiefland without stopping and continued on U.S. 27A until I reached FL 320 about a mile north. There I turned west and followed the signs to the Manatee Springs State Park, a spot that made me glad I had not spent more time at Blue Springs Park.

The most prominent feature at Manatee Springs State Park is a first-magnitude spring with some 117 million gallons of freshwater flowing from it every day. That's over 81,000 gallons a minute rising from beneath the surface and flowing into the Suwannee River. Of the 300 accessible springs in Florida, 27 are classified as first magnitude (at least 60 million gallons per day), and another 70 are classified as second magnitude (at least 6.5 million gallons per day).

The water is as clear as that in a swimming pool and a constant 72 degrees, but there's no blue plastic lining beneath these clear waters. Instead, there are limestone ledges along the outer edges of the boil (where the water rises from limestone caverns far beneath the ground's surface), and a deep drop into darkness at the boil itself.

I joined others who were swimming in the spring (you have to register with the park officials if you wish to scuba dive or snorkel) and swam around the edge of the pool and across the surface at the boil, where I could feel the incessant pressure generated by the water pushing its way to the surface. Then I decided to explore where the water went after it reached the surface.

I discovered that the park included much more than the spring. From a boardwalk along the 1,200-foot spring run (the water flow from the spring to the nearby river), I got an unobstructed view

of the water in the run and of the river swamp, where the trees were draped with Spanish moss and blooming air plants, or bromeliads.

Manatees, the large, gentle marine mammals that many believe provided mariners with the basis of the mermaid legend, used to gather at the spring boil during the cold weather, when the temperature of the Gulf of Mexico dropped. In recent years only one or two manatees have shown up each fall and winter, but the park still has plenty of other wildlife.

As I walked along the run and hiked the two marked trails in the 2,075-acre park, I saw white-tailed deer and a myriad of wading birds in the various plant communities. The latter included a swamp with cypress, gum, ash, and maple near the river; and a sand-hill community with pine and mixed hardwoods in the upland area of the park.

Other visitors were canoeing on the run and the river, most in the rental canoes that are available at the park concession during the spring, summer, and early fall. I considered renting one myself and venturing out into the Suwannee River, but didn't. What was really tempting me was to canoe the 23 miles from the park to the Gulf of Mexico, and I was afraid that I might attempt just that if I got into a canoe.

Resisting such an impulsive move, I left the park and continued on the road to the gulf. I returned to Chiefland on FL 320 and turned west on FL 345 in town. I later discovered that there are some back roads that cross from FL 320 near the park to FL 347 near Fowler Bluff. You can ask at the park for directions to these.

After going through about three miles of level farmland, I took a right on FL 347 to head toward Fowler Bluff and the banks of the Suwannee River. This route took me from level farmland to what is an anomaly in Florida, especially coastal Florida: hills. Not that they were high hills, mind you, but they were hills.

About five miles from FL 345 on FL 347 I came to Fowler Bluff, a small village with a bait shop and market on the banks of the Suwannee River, where I learned about the Lower Suwannee National Wildlife Refuge. This 50,000-acre refuge, which fronts 26 miles of the Gulf of Mexico, is in reality a hunting refuge, and nonhunters should be aware of the vast number of hunters that come there. At the refuge headquarters, about five miles south of Fowler Bluff, you can find out if it's currently open season for any type of hunting.

When I stopped by the headquarters, I discovered there were few open roads into the refuge, although there were a number of spots where I could park along the highway and walk in along sandy roads that are opened for hunters during the various seasons. The rangers also told me of the mile-long River Trail, which winds through hardwood swamps to the banks of the historic Suwannee River less than a mile back up the road toward Fowler Bluff, and of a county park within the refuge toward its southern end.

I headed back to the River Trail, where I walked alone beneath tall hardwood trees and through swamp to the river. Bird life was plentiful all along the trail, and I easily imagined that I was wandering through forests that few humans had invaded. John Muir must have felt much the same as he explored this region on his 1,000-mile walk to the gulf in 1869, only a few years after the end of the Civil War.

After exploring the River Trail, I headed back down FL 347 for about 10 miles. Then I turned west on FL 326 and continued into the refuge for just over three miles on a sandy road. This might be a difficult drive after a heavy rain, but it was easy in dry weather. The road took me through scrub growth on both sides of the road, past a hunters' campground operated by the county (a primitive campground with no amenities other than flat ground where hunters can park their campers and pitch their tents), and finally to Shell Mound County Park.

This small park protects a five-acre *midden* (garbage dump to modern humans) made entirely of shells discarded by Native Americans who lived here for several thousand years before Columbus reached America. Today vegetation covers this pile of shells, which reaches over 30 feet high in spots (the highest natural hill in the region is 52 feet). I took the self-guiding trail that winds around the mound to the gulf, where there is a view over the vast saltwater marsh surrounding Suwannee Sound.

I was alone on the trail, and this led to a heart-pounding moment when I walked around a curve into a bunch of land crabs that quickly scattered off the trail. The movement and accompanying rattling sounds startled me until I realized their origin. It was early October when I was there, and the fall butterfly migration was in full force. Beautiful swatches of color constantly flitted across the trail and settled onto low-lying vegetation at every turn.

After exploring about a mile of trail, I returned to the car to head for the final destination of this trip, Cedar Key. Retracing my steps to FL 347 and turning south, I had no plans of stopping before I reached the keys, but was intrigued by the signs for the Cedar Key Scrub State Preserve about a mile before FL 24. I parked on a sandy road that led into the preserve and hiked for a ways into the tranquil scrub, where the endangered Florida scrub jay abounds. The 4,000-acre preserve does not have outstanding beauty, but it is one of the few remaining undisturbed scrub cedar thickets along the Gulf Coast. I could have walked for several miles here, and fully intend to on my next visit to the area, but time was running short, and I wanted to get to Cedar Key.

After I turned right toward the keys at FL 24, the scrub continued alongside the road for another several miles. About four miles past the junction of FL 347 and FL 24, I came to the first bridge of the three-mile causeway that connects Cedar Key with the mainland. Cedar Key is the only community on the more than 100 small islands that form Cedar Keys, and the town is officially on Way Key. The rest of the islands are uninhabited except by thousands of birds, an unbelievable number of cottonmouth moccasins (snakes), plus plenty of alligators. The Cedar Keys National Wildlife Refuge comprises three of the larger keys (Seashore, Snake, and North). It is estimated that there is an average of 20 cottonmouths per acre on them. With residents such as that, who wants to visit, much less live, there?

One of my first impressions as I entered Cedar Key was that it had hills—not just rolling dunes but real hills. These give the town a feeling very different from that of most barrier island towns of the state, yet there was no doubt that I was in a Florida coastal community as I drove through downtown on a reconnaissance tour.

The old buildings had large windows and doors that opened onto covered balconies and porches, giving residents access to what cool breezes floated in off the gulf during the dog days of summer, and they all had the slightly run-down look common to weathered wood-frame buildings in the tropics.

My first stop was the Cedar Key Historical Society Museum, where I was introduced to the stormy (pun intended) history of the community. The area was settled in the early 1840s (when several of the keys had small communities), and Cedar Key became a thriving port city. A cross-state railroad reached the community in 1861, during the early stages of the Civil War. Union soldiers captured the port in 1862 to cut off the supply route for war materials that the Confederacy had developed, and the war-based economy ground to a halt. The community rebounded after the war, however, as the local pine and cypress were cut and shipped north, and local cedar was used to manufacture pencils in factories that were built on Way Key. This boom lasted until the 1880s; by that time Cedar Key was the second-largest city in Florida.

After the forests were depleted, the residents turned to the sea for oysters and fish, but several devastating hurricanes destroyed almost everything on the keys except the spirit of the residents. By the 1920s, Cedar Key's population had dropped below 1,000, and it now stands at about 900 residents.

The endurance and resilience of the residents has long given the community a quiet charm that was evident as I walked around the historic district. Most of the homes and buildings were well maintained (although weather-beaten) and lived in, but lacked the look of a restored area. They were what they were. Cedar Key has not been hit by such an influx of tourists that the old buildings have become something to see. Rather, they are unpretentiously maintained simply because they are in use.

Frame houses with tin roofs dominate the downtown, but as I drove by the schoolhouse on the way to the Cedar Key State Museum, I saw many brick and concrete-block homes that had been built in the past 40 years. In fact, they were much like homes that I had seen in small towns all across Florida.

Reaching the top of a hill, I stopped at a small cemetery, where the headstones told of the long and tortured history of the community; then I continued to the state museum, which tells about the history of the keys before Europeans came to Florida and about John Muir's 1,000-mile walk to the gulf from the upper Midwest in 1869. The museum has an excellent shell collection. From photos in the museum I could see that the downtown area hasn't changed dramatically since Muir's time, except that the larger buildings have been demolished by the powerful hurricanes that have swept over the keys in the past century.

I returned downtown and to the dock area to walk around, and found the genteel Island Hotel. This hand-hewn cypress building, dating from 1861, has withstood the ravages

Island Hotel, Cedar Key

of both time and ferocious hurricanes very well. That is not to say that it doesn't have its worn edges, but I felt very comfortable sitting in the same lobby, with its potbellied stove and church-pew benches, where Pearl Buck had sat on her visits to Cedar Key while working on some of her books. The hotel is listed in the National Register of Historic Places, and the antique furniture that fills all 10 guest rooms—plus the lobby, bar, and dining room—lends credence to that designation. The rooms have few modern conveniences (although all have air-conditioning to help guests cope with the enervating summer heat), and occasionally potential guests balk at the lack of private baths in some rooms. None quarrel, however, with the mosquito netting that drapes over the beds and comes in handy when the air-conditioning can be left off and the windows left open to capture the cooling ocean breezes in the spring and fall. The restaurant at the hotel serves gourmet natural dishes, but passes on serving palm salad (a standard at most restaurants in town) to help preserve the state tree.

Just up the street from the hotel are several arts-and-crafts shops that display the work of local artists as well as those who spend time on the keys during the year. As with

Key West in earlier years, Cedar Key has a small but thriving artists' colony, and the Chamber of Commerce sponsors the Cedar Key Sidewalk Arts Festival in April to feature their work.

As I walked farther from downtown toward the dock I reached an area that indicated that modern tourism was encroaching on this isolated community. The 30 modern, luxury condo units of The Island Place stand in sharp contrast to the weather-beaten buildings that line Main Street, offering the modern amenities that today's tourists seem to demand. I hoped that they stood empty and would slowly deteriorate to the general ambience of the rest of town before guests filled them, but I knew this was a futile dream.

The dock area maintains its fishing-village atmosphere, however, and there you can rent boats to row about the shallow waters around the key or ride the Island Hopper ferry to Seashore Key, the largest of the three keys in the Cedar Keys National Wildlife Refuge. To protect the 50,000 to 100,000 birds that live on the island (and remember that there are an average of 20 cottonmouth moccasins per acre in the interior), only the beaches are open to the public, but birders can enjoy the thrill of viewing so many birds. Shell fanciers don't mind that they can't go to the interior of the island, for the beaches of Seashore Key are some of the finest shelling beaches in Florida. The general lack of direct land access to the beaches has much to do with that. Most of the boats docked at Cedar Key are working fishing boats. In mid-October the annual Seafood Festival is held to celebrate, and taste, their harvests.

Return to Gainesville on FL 24 after a day of exploring the sights of Florida's Nature Coast. From Cedar Key to Otter Creek (at the junction of FL 24 and U.S. 19/98), the highway takes you through country with no buildings and very little chance to explore off the road. Most of the land on both sides of the route is swampland with slash pine rising from the black water, but the open areas on the road's right-of-way offer nature lovers an excellent opportunity to view birds and wildflowers. Wading and water-loving birds such as kingfishers are abundant here during times of high water; during the spring and most of the summer, wildflowers bloom profusely on the road banks just above the water level.

For More Information

Florida Museum of Natural History (Gainesville): 352-392-1721

Manatee Springs State Park (Chiefland): 904-493-6072

Lower Suwannee National Wildlife Refuge (Chiefland): 904-493-0238

Cedar Key Scrub State Preserve (Chiefland): 904-543-5567

Cedar Keys National Wildlife Refuge (Chiefland): 904-493-0238

Cedar Key Historical Society Museum (Cedar Key): 904-543-5549

Cedar Key State Museum (Cedar Key): 904-543-5350

Island Hotel (Cedar Key): 904-543-5111

Cedar Key Chamber of Commerce (Cedar Key): 904-543-5600

Cedar Key Sidewalk Arts Festival (Cedar Key): 904-543-5600

The Island Place (Cedar Key): 904-543-5307

Island Hopper Ferry (Cedar Key): 904-543-5904

Seafood Festival (Cedar Key): 904-543-5600

7

Eustis to Palatka

Getting there: From Orlando, take FL 437 northwest about 35 miles to Eustis and the start of this trip. From Eustis, take FL 19 north, through Altoona and Pittman, to Palatka. Reverse the route to return to Orlando.

Highlights: Lake Eustis, Ocala National Forest, Lake George, Hopkins Prairie, Henry H. Buckman Locks, Ravine State Gardens, St. Mark's Episcopal Church, Bronson-Mulholland House.

This trip begins in Eustis, where you will find Lake Eustis, the Clifford Taylor House, and the Waterman Hospital, which towers over downtown.

North of Eustis you enter the Ocala National Forest, where you see Lake George, Hopkins Prairie, and the Henry H. Buckman Locks.

The trip ends in Palatka—home to the Ravine State Gardens, with 100,000 azaleas and two swinging bridges; the St. Mark's Episcopal Church; and the Bronson-Mulholland House.

This one-day trip is 65 miles one-way.

Eustis is a small town (population 13,000). It once was part of a thriving citrus-growing region, but the severe freeze at Christmas 1983 devastated the groves. The few fruit trees I saw still standing in abandoned groves as I entered town were gray and decaying, but Eustis itself has sprung back from the disaster to become a prosperous community.

In downtown Eustis I stopped to walk in what residents call The Village, an old section of town where two streets have been redone to form a mall in which autos are not allowed. The old business section was built along the shore of Lake Eustis, and that is where smaller businesses still thrive. The shopping malls and supermarkets are found along U.S. 441, south of the old section. I walked around the rest of the old district and passed by Ferran's, which had a sign outside that shouted, "The Store with Squeaky Floors." It turned out to be a well-stocked dry-goods store that retains the ambience of an earlier era, when shoppers had plenty of time to sit on low stools while looking for the right pattern or hat, and the clerks knew everyone who came into the store. Ferran's still has its low stools and counters, and is as inviting as it must have been in years gone by.

The unusually large Waterman Hospital, which towers over downtown, looks more like a hotel than a hospital. It should. Frank Waterman, who was once head of the Waterman Fountain Pen Company, spent many winters in Eustis; he built the Fountain Inn there in the early 1920s to house the influx of tourists coming to the region. The hotel did well until the Depression years, when it was forced to close for lack of guests. Waterman then gave the building to the city for use as a hospital, and it's now the largest in the region, serving more than 20,000 patients annually.

Also near the lakefront, the Bay Street Players perform stage productions in a restored movie theater, and the historical society has a museum in the Clifford Taylor House, a two-story mansion built in 1910–11.

After walking around Eustis I continued north toward Umatilla and Altoona on FL 19. About 10 miles north of Eustis, I came to Lake Dorr and the small community of Pittman. The Ocala National Forest, the oldest national forest east of the Mississippi and the southernmost national forest in the United States, begins about two miles south of Pittman, and I visited the Ocala National Forest Pittman Visitor Center across the road from Lake Dorr (about two miles north of Altoona).

At the visitors center I learned of dozens of recreational activities in the national forest, but I was particularly interested in those I could explore on or near FL 19. The forest was obviously well harvested, and had the appearance of a tree farm rather than of the national forests that I am used to in the Far West. I learned at the center that it is the most heavily harvested national forest in Florida, producing more than four times more timber each year than the combined harvests of the Osceola and Apalachicola national forests farther north.

While this heavy harvest detracts somewhat from the wildness of the forests along FL 19, there is plenty of wild land left. The forest covers more than 430,000 acres, and is home to a  wide variety of birds and other wildlife, including about 200 Florida black bears. Almost 40 active bald eagle nests have also been identified there.

Driving north from Pittman I passed FL 445, which would have taken me to Alexander Springs (about five miles to the east), and then FL 40, which would have taken me to Juniper Springs (to the west). I bypassed both of these, since I had seen many springs during my travels in Florida, but can recommend either of them if you haven't visited a spring. They both have interpretive centers and nature trails.

About five miles past the intersection with FL 40, I reached the western shore of Lake George, the second largest lake in

Florida and home to most of the wintering bald eagles in the Ocala National Forest. I was not lucky enough to spot any while I was driving by, but if you visit the area between December and April, you are likely to see nesting eagles around the shore of the lake, and more eagles feeding over it.

To the west of the road along this section were prime examples of the "Big Scrub" that covers major portions of the central ridge of Florida. This region consists of gently rolling hills with stands of sand pine and turkey scrub oak, and parts of the movie adapted from Marjorie K. Rawlings's novel *The Yearling* were filmed here. Rawlings herself lived to the northwest of the national forest, and used the setting for several of her books. The scrub is delicate and continuously struggling to survive, but despite the considerable logging in the Ocala National Forest, large areas of the scrub such as the country to the west of Lake George, have been left relatively unscathed over the years thanks to the unproductive nature of the land and its general inaccessibility.

Near the northern end of Lake George, and about 10 miles north of FL 40, I saw signs to Hopkins Prairie. Prairies in Florida are somewhat different from most people's idea of how a prairie should look. Florida prairies are just as likely to be water-covered depressions in the midst of scrub growth or upland forests as they are grass-covered open land. More frequently they are a combination of the two. During and just after the wet season, water stands knee-high among the tall grasses, but as the region enters the dry season, the water evaporates, and it becomes possible to walk across wide stretches of land that were covered with water only weeks earlier.

I drove over a sandy but well-maintained road about three miles to Hopkins Prairie and the depths of the scrub thicket. There was a primitive campground near the prairie that was obviously used by hunters, but no one was using any of the campsites when I visited.

The prairie itself looked much as I had imagined it when I had read *The Yearling* as a youngster. The scrub suddenly gave way to a wide open space that appeared to be covered with grass, but upon closer inspection I discovered that a thin covering of water kept me from exploring what I had thought to be open meadow.

I did explore around the edge of the water, however, and saw many small birds, some deer, and raptors soaring overhead. Anyone traveling this route with an RV might want to stop overnight here, especially if it is not hunting season, for many small mammals such as raccoons, opossum, bobcats, and sometimes even the elusive black bear and Florida panther come to the water's edge to feed and drink. If you are lucky, you may see some of them on a moonlit night.

After stopping at Hopkins Prairie, I continued up FL 19 and enjoyed long stretches of dense forests that lined both sides of the road. Lake George is only one of a series of lakes that sits astride the St. Johns River, which wends its way to the Atlantic at Jacksonville. About 15 miles north of Hopkins Prairie I saw signs leading to the Henry H. Buckman Locks to the east of FL 19. I could tell from the signs that this was a U.S. Army Corps of Engineers project, but had no idea what the project was.

I drove over a well-maintained asphalt road for about two miles to the locks, and there learned about an aborted attempt in the middle part of this century to build a cross-Florida canal. The idea was to use the St. Johns River, which is navigable to Palatka some five miles downstream, as the entrance to a canal that would take barges across Florida from Jacksonville to the Gulf Coast. A canal, complete with locks, was cut from the St. Johns to Lake Ocklawaha (behind Rodman Dam on Ocklawaha River). Plans called for it to continue on across the peninsula.

Conservationists realized the potential for ecological damage from such a project and, with the help of fiscally conservative legislators in both Tallahassee and Washington, finally stopped the project. But this was only after extensive work on the canal had been done and the locks on the St. Johns completed. Looking out over the locks, I couldn't help wondering at the folly of public projects around the nation. In San Francisco, near where I live, an unfinished freeway leading to nowhere stood over the Embarcadero for several decades before the 1989 Loma Prieta earthquake damaged it enough that it was torn down, and here in central Florida were locks that led to nowhere and were being maintained by the Corps of Engineers long after any need for the locks existed. After looking at the locks, I returned to FL 19 and headed into Palatka, the end point of this trip.

Palatka sits in a large S-bend where the St. Johns River is over a mile wide. The town was the center of a thriving lumber industry prior to the Civil War, and was occupied by Union troops during the conflict. After the war it became a fashionable winter resort, with tourists coming from the cold Northeast by train to Jacksonville, and then continuing upriver to Palatka by steamboat. By the end of the 19th century there were nine resort hotels in town, including the Putnam House with 400 rooms.

Today Palatka is a quiet town that has been bypassed as a major tourist center; now its chief claim to fame is that it is the "Bass Fishing Capital of the World." There are attractions there, however, and none is more colorful than the Ravine State Gardens just south of town. The garden was a Works Progress Administration (WPA) project during the 1930s, when some 70,000 azaleas were planted on the hillsides of three large ravines formed by sinkholes in the limestone. Each February and March more than 100,000 camellias and azaleas burst into brilliant bloom, and you can enjoy the display by foot or car.

A three-mile drive circles around the rim of the ravines, and several miles of paths take you down into the lush canyons. There you may walk across swinging bridges, gaze at miniature waterfalls and rock formations, or just enjoy the moss, ferns, jasmine, and banana trees. There were no blooms to enjoy when I was there, but I still had a good time strolling along the paths and exploring the park. I discovered that you must be careful on the swinging bridges—once they begin to swing, they don't stop until you are off.

In town I discovered the refurbished river district, with its Riverfront Walk and Park, and enjoyed a break while watching boats on the river. It wasn't time for dinner, or I would have tried one of the many restaurants that have opened along the riverfront, but I did browse in the shops and boutiques before I headed to the Bronson-Mulholland House, a restored, three-story, plantation-style house built of cypress that is open to the public on certain days. The Greek Revival–style house was built for Judge Isaac Bronson, a major political figure in Florida in the late 19th century.

Just before reaching the mansion, I drove by the St. Mark's Episcopal Church. This church was designed by Richard Upjohn, architect of New York's Trinity Church, and built in the 1850s. Union troops used it as a shelter during the Civil War. Although it is not open to the public, it is an interesting building that you may want to look at as you head to the Bronson-Mulholland House, which was the last stop on my trip.

Return to Orlando by the same route.

For More Information

Eustis Chamber of Commerce (Eustis): 904-357-3434

Bay Street Players (Eustis): 904-357-7777

Clifford Taylor House (Eustis): 904-483-0046

Ocala National Forest, Seminole Ranger District (Eustis): 904-357-3721

Ocala National Forest Pittman Visitor Center (Pittman): 904-669-7495

Henry H. Buckman Locks (Palatka): 904-328-1690

Putnam County Chamber of Commerce (Palatka): 904-328-1503

Ravine State Gardens (Palatka): 904-329-3721

Bronson-Mulholland House (Palatka): 904-329-0140

8

Land O'Lakes to Inverness

Getting there: From Tampa, head north for 10 miles on U.S. 41 to Land O'Lakes and the starting point for this trip. Continue north on U.S. 41 to Masaryktown, Brooksville, and Floral City. Take Old Floral City Road north to Inverness. To return to Tampa, reverse the route, or head east to I-75 and take I-75 south to Tampa.

Highlights: Hernando Heritage Museum, Annual Brooksville Raid Reenactment, Chinsegut National Wildlife Refuge, Withlacoochee State Forest, Fort Cooper, Crown Hotel.

From Land O'Lakes to Masaryktown you drive through sparsely populated areas with slash pine rising from blackwater swamps.

Past Masaryktown you leave the low-lying swamps, and the terrain rises slowly as you approach the farmland around Brooksville. In that town you'll find Rogers' Christmas House, the Hernando Heritage Museum, and Dade Battlefield.

After Brooksville you'll pass by the Chinsegut National Wildlife Refuge; Withlacoochee State Forest, with its hiking trails; and Fort Cooper. The route ends in Inverness with the Crown Hotel.

This day trip is about 55 miles one-way.

Heading north from Tampa, U.S. 41 goes from the urban center of one of the largest cities in Florida, through slightly rundown suburbs, to a depressed rural area around Land O'Lakes, all within 10 miles. In many ways I went through a time change as I drove along this route, and felt as though I had returned to my home in the Deep South during the late 1940s and early 1950s. Early travelers took a stage from Tampa to Brooksville, Inverness, and Ocala along what is now U.S. 41, and the road remained the primary route to northern Florida for many years until I-75 was completed. Today's travelers bypass most of the route as they journey northward on the wide and speedy interstate, but those who choose to take a more leisurely trip will find U.S. 41 an interesting alternative that leads through old Florida.

As I reached Land O'Lakes I expected to find a country community, but instead found little more than a couple of businesses. There is no town center; the name itself was determined in the 1950s when school and postal service consolidation required that the many small surrounding communities decide upon a name for the new post office.

The communities in the region have been in a holding pattern for years, and residents squeak out a subsistence living by working in the remaining forests and fishing in the gulf. Earlier times were little more affluent, but there had been spurts of economic activity in the late 1800s as logging and turpentine interests provided at least seasonal jobs for those living in the blackwater swamps that form the headwaters of the Anclote River.

As I drove farther north, I saw that little had changed for most of those who lived in the area now. Prosperity was at best relative and then only a fleeting and seasonal occurrence. Boats were standard fixtures in the yards of most homes close to the road (and no doubt of those hidden behind the growths of slash pine and live oak as well); most looked heavily used, unlike many boats that are berthed at slips around Tampa and St. Petersburg. These were working boats, not pleasure ones, and the catch from them was an important part of the families' subsistence.

Both homes and businesses along the route were weather-worn, and many had been deserted—left unattended to weather the passing of time. Most of the deserted buildings and many of the inhabited ones were decorated with "For Sale" signs, some of which were almost as weatherbeaten as the buildings they were advertising.

I found the stretch of road between Land O'Lakes and Masaryktown depressingly similar to backwater regions all over the South, where prosperity is just down the road in distance but far away in time. Nevertheless, the beauty of the landscape enticed me to the side of the road at times. There I would gaze at fields being encroached upon by live oaks covered with Spanish moss that draped to the ground or at an opening in the slash pines that rose from the swamps, where I might spot an alligator's head or a turtle sunning itself on a log. Wherever I looked, though, there was little room to explore or move, and I knew that local residents must have shared my feelings of being hemmed in. The unending resistance of nature kept humans at bay here, and it was only through persistence and perseverance that even a subsistence living could be earned.

The residents obviously sought hope through religion, for there was a multitude of small, often run-down, churches along the highway. The only other establishments that may have outnumbered the churches were the used-car lots (frequently combined with junkyards and/or garages) that lined the route.

Things began to change as I reached Masaryktown. The land was a little higher—not a lot but just enough to make it less confining—and it seemed that the residents had made more headway in their attempt to survive. Not that it had been that much easier than it was in the lower-lying region

just to the south, but more homes were congregated together and there seemed to be more of a sense of community than in the other small settlements that I had passed earlier. Masaryktown was the brainchild of Czechoslovakian immigrant and New York City newspaper editor Joseph Joscak. With the help of other immigrants, Joscak formed the Hernando Plantation Company to purchase land and develop the town in the early 1900s, and during the boom years of the 1920s, many Czech immigrants found their way to the settlement.

Today the dominant building in the community is the Masaryktown Hotel, which was built in 1926 to serve as a rooming house for the people building their homes and soon became the social center of the community. Although it is no longer used as a hotel, its restaurant is known throughout Florida for its fine Czech food.

A canning plant was built in town in the early 1930s, but after several freezes destroyed the citrus groves that had been planted in the area, poultry replaced citrus as the primary industry. Egg production expanded through the Depression, the Second World War, and until 1960, when four days and nights of rain wiped out over 30,000 chickens and devastated the region's poultry producers. Egg production bounced back for a while, but today there are few egg producers left in the region. In fact, there appears to be little employment of any kind in the area.

Through all these trials one thing has survived, however: the community's strong identification with its Czech heritage. Each year the residents celebrate three Czechoslovakian events: the founding of the town, Czechoslovakian Independence Day, and the birthday of Thomas Garrigue Masaryk, a resistance leader during World War I and the first president of the newly created Czechoslovakia after the war ended. All of these celebrations include good food, dancing, and other ethnic activities.

As I left Masaryktown, U.S. 41 continued to rise from the low-lying swamps to higher land, and prosperity seemed to come with the gain in elevation. The rolling hills between Garden Grove Estates and Brooksville were covered with open pastures full of horses, and surrounded by green fields of hay.

Brooksville is the largest town in Hernando County and the primary shopping center for a large farming region. The town sits amid several moderate-size hills, and I sought out the Hernando County Chamber of Commerce to see what might be of interest there. Rogers' Christmas House and Village, the most popular attraction in town, is in a 10-room house and several adjoining buildings. You'll find on display (and for sale) what the owners claim is the largest selection of Christmas ornaments in the country. While some of the ornaments are tasteful, there are plenty that will satisfy even the most gauche of shoppers. Anyone interested in a string of Holstein Christmas-tree lights? For those who are, the Christmas House and Village is open every day of the year except Christmas.

The Hernando Heritage Museum, located in a four-story house that was built sometime in the 1850s, was much more interesting. After many years of neglect, the house was empty and sorely in need of attention when the Hernando Historical Museum Association was formed in 1981. Since then the building has been restored, and each of the 12 rooms has been refurbished to reflect an important period of Hernando County's history.

While I was touring the delightful exhibits, I learned about the major fund-raiser for the museum association, the Annual Brooksville Raid Reenactment. Each January, Civil War buffs from around the country come to the Dade Battlefield outside

Brooksville to faithfully reenact the series of small skirmishes that took place between Union and Confederate troops just outside Brooksville during the war. I was not there during a reenactment, but this annual event is said to be one of the most faithful renditions of a Civil War battle of all those held in the nation.

I continued north on U.S. 41 after I toured the museum, and about five miles out of town took a left on County 491 to head toward the Chinsegut National Wildlife Refuge. I didn't know what to expect along this side trip. In actuality I saw little, since the refuge was closed to visitors except along the shores of Lake Lindsey. I could tell, however, that there was one time of year when the trip would have been spectacular. There were thick stands of dogwood trees along the road, and during the spring blooming season the large white blossoms must stand out in brilliant contrast against the green background of new leaves.

At the junction of County 491 and 476, I stopped at the Lake Lindsey Grocery, a remnant of earlier times when rural grocery stores provided isolated communities with social gathering spots as well as places to purchase staples. I bought only a soft drink but could have found out about the fishing at Lake Lindsey, when the refuge was open to visitors, or any other small bit of knowledge that these social centers still provide residents and outsiders.

I turned right on County 476 to head back to U.S. 41, and followed along the north side of the refuge for most of the way. To the north of the road was open farmland, which was a marked contrast to the thickly wooded refuge to the south.

At the intersection with County 476, I crossed over U.S. 41 to pick up a local delicacy: green, hot boiled peanuts. These may not be to everyone's taste, but they have been a favorite of mine since I was child in Mississippi. You will see these advertised on the side of the road all over northern

Florida. Some areas even have specialty items, such as Cajun-flavored boiled peanuts.

After buying my snack I headed north on U.S. 41. Just past County 581 I noticed a sign to the Colonel Robins Nature Trail of the Withlacoochee State Forest. Since I had not been able to explore the wildlife refuge, I stopped to find out more about the natural history of the area. I soon realized that in the past several miles I had entered a very different ecological community than what I had passed through at the refuge. There were no dense groves of hardwoods to explore here; instead, I was in a pine upland that was gradually changing, through natural progression, into a hardwood forest.

There are three loop trails at the site. The north loop is .8 mile long, the south loop .75 mile, and the lower loop one mile. I walked all three self-guided loops for a total of just over 2.5 miles, and thoroughly enjoyed the markers that told how the suppression of fire during the last half century had led to the growth of hardwoods that will gradually gain dominance over the pine in the forest. Even if you don't take the entire walk, this is a good place to stop for a short break and maybe for a walk on one of the shorter trails. You may also want to visit two other nature trails in the forest. These are the McKeathan Lake Nature Trail, just off U.S. 41 seven miles north of Brooksville, and the Citrus Hiking Trail, to the west of Inverness.

I returned to U.S. 41 and continued north to Floral City. In Brooksville I had been told not to miss the drive from Floral City to Inverness along the Old Floral City Road. So I turned off U.S. 41 onto FL 48 and headed for downtown Floral City, where huge oaks form a high canopy over the road. The Spanish moss hangs down in wisps that further filter what sunlight makes it through the oak canopy. I didn't find a more scenic side trip in all my travels through Florida.

After I drove through downtown, I turned north on Old Floral City Road and headed toward Inverness, but had one more stop before I reached the end of this trip. This was Fort Cooper State Park, which is off Old Floral City Road just south of Inverness.

Florida has been contested territory since the first Europeans arrived there in the 1500s, and plenty of parks and memorials around the state commemorate battles in a wide variety of wars. Fort Cooper was from one of the more obscure wars, the Second Seminole War, which was fought in the late 1830s.

General Winfield Scott led a long march across mid-Florida toward Tampa in 1836, and built a small compound and fort on the shores of Lake Holathlikaha, where he left Major Mark Anthony Cooper in charge of 380 sick and wounded men. The men held firm in the fort for 16 days until Scott returned with supplies and reinforcements. The first weekend in March the excavated fort is now the site of a reenactment of those long-ago events. Volunteers and park personnel gather to share information about the period and to reenact skirmishes from the war.

I found the park an attractive and interesting one even without the reenactments, as I walked along some of the 10-plus miles of trails. As they crisscross the 710-acre park from the lakeshore, to the woodlands with many hardwoods, to the sand-hill community of dry open forests, the trails are an excellent route from which to observe the flora and fauna of central Florida's rolling hills. After hiking without taking time out for lunch, I was ready for something special once I reached Inverness—and did I find it!

I stopped by the Citrus County Chamber of Commerce to pick up brochures and pamphlets about Citrus County, but all the clerks were busy, so I didn't ask any questions about Inverness (population 6,000). I figured that I could find out all I needed to know simply by walking around. I had passed the old courthouse, built in 1912, on the way into town, and thought I would work my way back to it on the side streets.

I never made it, for I almost immediately walked into a sight that I never expected to find in rural Florida. Standing around the corner from the chamber was the Crown Hotel, a very impressive structure that impressed me even more as I entered.

The hotel was built in the 1890s as Inverness's first general store, and was later converted into a hotel during World War I. Although it had been moved, split in two, and added onto between 1920 and 1979, it had not been generally renovated or restored when British investor Reg Brealy bought the run-down building for $100,000 in 1979.

Brealy invested another $2.3 million to transform the old building into a deluxe, elegant, English-style country inn with a Victorian-era ambience. The present manager, Scotsman Ian Young, said, "It's the last place in Florida you'd expect to find a hotel like this." From the glass-encased replicas of the crown jewels in the lobby to the bedrooms with brass beds and Chippendale furnishings to the antique double-decker bus that sits out front, everything says "British Isles." Even the Fox and Hounds Tavern, which offers steak and kidney pie and fish and chips, asks that you dress appropriately. I never found out what that meant, for I was most definitely inappropriate with my sweaty and dusty hiking attire, so I opted to go elsewhere.

I saw many interesting and impressive hotels and inns during my travels around Florida, but if I had just one place in the state to take my wife for a romantic weekend, it would be hard to pass on the Crown Hotel, with its quiet hospitality, special packages, and highly acclaimed Churchill Restaurant.

Return to Tampa by the same route, or head east to I-75 for a faster return trip.

For More Information

Masaryktown Hotel (Masaryktown): 904-796-1087

Hernando County Chamber of Commerce (Brooksville):
904-796-2420

Rogers' Christmas House and Village (Brooksville):
904-796-2415

Hernando Heritage Museum (Brooksville): 904-799-0129

Withlacoochee State Forest (Brooksville): 904-796-5650

Cooper State Park (Inverness): 904-726-0315

Citrus County Chamber of Commerce (Inverness):
904-726-2801

Crown Hotel (Inverness): 904-344-5535

9

Eatonville to Mt. Dora

Getting there: From Orlando head north on I-4 for about 10 miles to the small town of Eatonville. From Eatonville return to I-4 and go north for 15 miles to FL 46. Turn west on FL 46 and go about 5 miles to the Lower Wekiva River State Preserve. From the preserve continue on FL 46 another 12 miles to Mt. Dora. Return to Orlando by the same route or by FL 441.

Highlights: Eatonville, Lower Wekiva River State Preserve, Sandhill Nature Trail, Mt. Dora.

The trip's first stop is at the all-black community of Eatonville, where you can visit the first incorporated black town in the United States. From there you head to an environmentally significant preserve along the banks of Black Water Creek and the St. Johns and Wekiva Rivers. The rest of the trip is spent in the resort town of Mt. Dora.

This day trip is about 45 miles one-way.

This route was something of an afterthought. While spending some free time in Orlando, I asked friends where would be a good place to spend a free day, and most of them pointed me north to Mt. Dora. Although I usually spend any free moments outdoors hiking or canoeing while in Florida, I decided to see some of historic Florida that reflected how the early years of tourism must have been. For that I couldn't have chosen a better spot than Mt. Dora.

I got an early start, and as I was fighting my way through rush hour traffic on I-4, I saw the exit to Eatonville, which struck a chord in my memory. Although I couldn't quite remember its importance, I left the freeway to see what was there.

What I found was a small community with little to see but a lot to absorb. Only about 3,000 residents call this 112-acre town their home, and they are all African Americans. Not that that should be unusual, since Eatonville was the first incorporated African American municipality in the United States, and is the proud birthplace of Zora Neale Hurston, an anthropologist and writer of note during the first half of the 20th century. She was friends with Langston Hughes and other artists of the Harlem Renaissance in the 1920s, and studied under such noted academics as anthropologist Franz Boas.

Eatonville annually honors its native daughter in January or February with the annual Zora Neale Hurston Festival of the Arts and Humanities, exhibiting works of black artists in the Zora Neale Hurston National Museum of Fine Arts, a small storefront on the town's main street. After learning about Eatonville and Hurston, I continued on my way and headed north on I-4 toward the larger town of Sanford, from which I headed west on FL 46.

The heavy development that I had been in since leaving Orlando suddenly left off as I headed west, and I was soon driving through uninhabited areas that seemed as though they had not been changed since the first Europeans settled the region. Although that wasn't so, I did come to the signs for the Lower Wekiva River State Preserve, where truly little has changed in the past 500 years. Along the banks of the St. Johns and Wekiva Rivers the state has preserved more than 4,600 acres of pristine plant communities that range from high, dry sand hills to river swampland.

I stopped at the trailhead for the Sandhill Nature Trail, which leads north from the highway and makes a loop through a good sampling of the plant communities protected in the preserve, and headed into the woods for a leisurely walk. And that is what I had, as I wandered along the winding trail with no hills to climb or obstacles to avoid. Birds flitted from tree to tree as squirrels chattered, and I could feel a slight breeze moving through the vegetation. At one turn I surprised a gopher tortoise grazing on wire grass. This large turtle is listed as a "species of special concern" in Florida because the deep, sandy soils where the animals build their homes is also attractive to human developers in the state. I considered myself fortunate to have seen one in its natural habitat.

The walk took about an hour, after which I returned to the car for the drive to Mt. Dora, where to my surprise I discovered that there actually is a mount—or at least a semblance of one. With rolling hills, perfectly manicured homes amid dark-green lawns rimmed with blooms, and even a lighthouse on the shores of Lake Dora, you couldn't ask for a more perfect setting for a romantic getaway.

In fact, the town has been compared to a quiet New England village in ambience, and certainly seems much closer to that than to the modern world of Orlando, only half an hour south. The streets are lined with hundreds of shops, antiques are found everywhere, and even man's best friend is not left out—Piglet's Pantry, a gourmet bakery for dogs, is found on East Fourth Avenue.

By the time I found Piglet's Pantry I was more interested in gourmet food for myself, however, and for that I headed down to the Lakeside Inn. This vintage Victorian structure was built in 1883, and continues to provide unsurpassed rooms and meals to meet the tastes of the most discerning traveler, as it has since it opened.

I sat on the front porch after a pleasant meal and looked out over Lake Dora, much as Calvin Coolidge had done when he spent his first winter here after leaving the White House. As I did, I saw one of the sightseeing boats that ply the waters of Lake Dora and nearby Lake Eustis, and remembered that Grantland Rice, a leading sportswriter of the 1920s and 1930s, called the Dora Canal, a natural stream connecting the two lakes, "the most beautiful mile of water in the world." Having been on one of the tours out of Tavares on Lake Eustis, I knew that the passengers were experiencing Florida at its best.

As I was leaving town I stopped by the Unity House, where I should have begun my visit. This turn-of-the-century home now contains the Mount Dora Historical Society, recounting the early years of the town.

Although I seldom make regular tourist destinations a priority when I travel, Mt. Dora is certainly one that I would return to if I needed a place to enjoy a relaxing weekend, and Eatonville was an unexpected addition to the day.

For More Information

Zora Neale Hurston Festival of the Arts and Humanities (Eatonville): 407-647-3307

Lower Wekiva River State Preserve (Sanford): 407-330-6728

Piglet's Pantry (Mt. Dora): 352-735-9779

The Lakeside Inn (Mt. Dora): 352-383-4101 or 800-556-5016

Dora Canal Tours (Tavares): 352-343-4337

Mount Dora Historical Society (Mt. Dora): 352-383-5228

10

Bradenton to Sebring

Getting there: Begin in Bradenton at the De Soto National Monument, which is located at the end of 57th Street. From Bradenton take FL 64 east to Zolfo Springs, then follow FL 66 east to FL 635. Take FL 635 north to Highlands Hammock State Park, and follow FL 634 to Sebring. Reverse the route to return to Bradenton.

Highlights: De Soto National Monument, South Florida Museum, Gamble Plantation State Historic Site, Manatee Village Historical Park, Pioneer Park, Highlands Hammock State Park, Sebring International Raceway.

After visiting the De Soto National Monument, stop at the South Florida Museum, the Gamble Plantation State Historic Site, and the Manatee Village Historical Park before heading east on FL 64.

FL 64 follows the old Cracker Trail from Bradenton across Florida toward Fort Pierce; the next stop is at the Lake Manatee State Recreation Area.

Continue on FL 64 through farming and ranching country to Zolfo Springs, where you can stop at Pioneer Park to see an old log cabin and a historical museum.

From Zolfo Springs take FL 66 to FL 635, then follow the signs to Highlands Hammock State Park. From the park, take FL 634 to the end of the route at Sebring.

This full-day trip is about 80 miles one-way.

Hernando de Soto is almost a patron saint to the residents of Manatee County on the west coast of Florida. He led one of the largest excursions ever organized by early Europeans to explore what was then called La Florida by the Spanish. He is purported to have landed at the mouth of the Manatee River in the spring of 1539 with an expedition that included 600 men, 500 horses, and provisions to last a month. De Soto traveled inland to the region where Ocala, Gainesville, and Tallahassee are now located before heading west to the Mississippi River, where he died of fever.

Each spring de Soto's landing is re-created at the De Soto National Monument, which is at the mouth of the Manatee River (about five miles west of downtown Bradenton). My first stop on this trip was at the monument. There, after watching a short film on de Soto's expedition, I wandered around the visitors center and museum and then visited the monument commemorating his landing. Although the park honors de Soto, it does provide an evenhanded appraisal of how his expedition affected the Native Americans who had lived in the region for thousands of years before he arrived.

As I followed along the De Soto Trail exhibit, I discovered the beginning of a half-mile nature trail that led out to De Soto Point, where the Manatee River enters the Gulf of Mexico. Along the beach I saw a number of seabirds, and as I wandered through the dense mangrove thicket, I could almost imagine myself one of the de Soto party wading ashore onto strange and unknown ground. Returning to the visitors center from the point, I passed a pile of what looked like broken concrete blocks, and found that they were the remains of a cabin built in the 1840s out of tabby—a pioneer concoction of sand, limestone, and shells that was indeed similar to concrete.

I returned toward downtown Bradenton on FL 64, and turned north at the corner of FL 64 and U.S. 41 to the South Florida Museum. This modern museum is dedicated to telling Florida's story from prehistoric times to the Space Age, which is apparent from its wide variety of exhibits and features including a planetarium, star shows, laser-light shows, and observatory. I bypassed these, however, and concentrated on the early-history exhibits. Period rooms gave me an excellent overview of lifestyles from earlier eras, and in the Spanish courtyard I explored replicas of 16th-century Spanish homes and chapels.

From the museum I continued north on U.S. 41 to Patten Avenue in Ellenton, where I stopped at the Gamble Plantation State Historic Site and Memorial to J. P. Benjamin. This antebellum structure sits on the site of a former sugar plantation and refinery that covered over 3,500 acres during its peak years, prior to the Civil War. A mansion, that has been painstakingly restored by the United Daughters of Confederacy and the Florida State Parks, it is an impressive structure and the only antebellum one to have survived in southern Florida.

Major Robert Gamble built the mansion (I should say he had his slaves build it) in 1844, while he was attempting to develop a successful sugar plantation. He never found financial success, however, and after falling almost $200,000 in debt, sold the plantation and returned to Tallahassee. The plantation never reached the level of production that Gamble had imagined, and it likely would have been left to rot away, as other antebellum homes were, but for a single event that prompted the United Daughters of Confederacy to acquire the property, restore it to its original opulence, and deed it to the Florida State Parks system.

In May 1865, as the Civil War ended, Judah P. Benjamin, one of the key men in the Confederate government and its secretary of state, used the house as a way station on his escape route to Great Britain. The United States had offered a reward of $50,000 in gold for Benjamin's capture, and Archibald McNeil, then owner of the Gamble Plantation, gave him sanctuary until his escape was arranged.

I couldn't keep from thinking that this must be an "only in America" story. Where else would there be a park and memorial, lovingly restored and maintained, that was devoted to someone who would now (and was then in the North) be considered a traitor? It did cause me to wonder about the meaning of patriotism, especially in a state where large American flags fly and residents frequently say, "Love it or leave it." In addition to the mansion, the 14 acres contain the Patten House, an 1890s farmhouse, and ruins of what was once one of the largest sugar mills in the South.

I retraced my route to Bradenton before heading east on FL 64. On my way out of town, I came to the Manatee Village Historical Park, which has six historic buildings that were moved to their present location to give people a better understanding of what life was like for early Florida settlers. The buildings date from 1860 through 1912, and include a courthouse, church, farmhouse, store, schoolhouse, and home. The Wiggins Store has a hands-on room, where children can wear period costumes and play with toys from the late 19th and early 20th centuries as they pretend they are living back then.

The home is a cracker-style house, which was appropriate since I was loosely following the old Florida Cracker Trail on its way across the state from Bradenton to Fort Pierce. No one is certain where the term *cracker* came from, but

the most accepted theory is that its origins are the cracking whips of early cowhands as they drove large herds of cattle across the peninsula. Today the cattle industry still thrives along the trail, but the cowhands no longer take herds on long drives.

As I drove along FL 64 I quickly left the congestion of the coast behind, and within 10 miles was in sparsely populated country. When I saw the sign for Lake Manatee State Recreation Area, I thought I would explore some of the open country.

The 2,400-acre reservoir on the Manatee River provides drinking water to the heavily populated coastal counties, but the land surrounding it has remained relatively unchanged over the years. Although the land has been used for everything from farming and cattle grazing to turpentining and timbering, the ecological communities there are intact.

I walked along several trails through sand and pine scrub, and around some depression marshes, and I saw many small birds and animals, but no people. Most visitors to the park come for the boating and fishing that the lake provides, and the trails are nearly devoid of people. This gave me a good feel for what the settlers must have seen and felt on their explorations in Florida's early years.

Back on the road, I continued along the Florida Cracker Trail across flat grazing land, where cattle ranching still reigns supreme, until I reached the small crossroads community of Zolfo Springs. I hadn't expected to find anything interesting there, so I was surprised, on following the signs to Pioneer Park, to discover a quiet little park on the banks of the Peace River.

Zolfo Springs began as a railroad boomtown in the late 1800s, when the Florida Southern Railroad came through. The town was named for a group of free-flowing sulfur springs nearby (they have long since been filled) that the

Italian railroad workers called "zolfo" for sulfur. Today little is left of the boomtown days, but in Pioneer Park I found an old-time blacksmith shop, the William Henry Hart cabin from 1879, and a locomotive from the same period. I didn't visit the nearby Cracker Museum, for it was closed (although according to the sign it should have been open). The museum supposedly has exhibits on the history of the region from the early Native Americans to the Florida Crackers.

Each year the Florida Cracker Trail Association sponsors an eight-day, 150-mile trail ride for equestrians in late April or early May, following the Florida Cracker Trail from Bradenton to Fort Pierce. The first part of the ride closely parallels FL 64 from Bradenton to Zolfo Springs.

From Zolfo Springs the trail ride follows FL 66, and I took this road as I headed toward Highlands Hammock State Park. The countryside continued to have remarkably little development and commercialization. Ranches and open prairie dominated the scenery, with an occasional orange grove to break the monotony of flat land with few trees. As I got closer to Sebring and Highlands Hammock, orange groves became more common and hardwood hammocks occasionally stood out against the horizon.

Before FL 66 ended at U.S. 27, I took a left turn and then headed north on FL 635 for four miles to Highlands Hammock State Park. This was one of the four original state parks that were created in Florida in 1935, and today its 3,800 acres are home to almost 200 species of birds, plenty of alligators and feral pigs, and diverse plant communities. In the marshes and swamps, for example, there are 60 species of native ferns.

I liked this park so much that I brought my family here on a follow-up trip to Florida, for it is an ideal family park. It has a campground, interpretive center, ranger-led tram tours, and eight short nature trails that cover a total of 3.5 miles. The land for the park was purchased in 1931 by Margaret S.

Roebling to preserve a virgin hardwood forest (called a hammock in Florida) from farm development. Today visitors frequently cite the Cypress Swamp Trail as the most memorable of the eight trails.

I followed the boardwalk as it led me above the black water of the cypress swamp, and eagerly searched for alligators as I went. I had heard stories of 12-foot ones that often sunned in open spots near the boardwalk, but was not fortunate enough to see one that day. I did see a young one about three feet long at the observation stop near the end of the boardwalk, but the ibises that startled me as much as I had startled them were the high point of the short hike. These large white wading birds were feeding in the shallow waters of the swamp. As I rounded a bend in the trail, a flock of about 10 of them rose with flapping wings and flew en masse across the boardwalk just ahead of me at head height.

I walked other trails that led through an ancient hammock, a young hammock, and a wild orange grove before I left the park to head on into Sebring, the end of this trip. Along the trails I saw feral pigs; in the trees I heard, then saw, a large pileated woodpecker; and in the sky overhead I observed several magnificent swallowtail kites hovering above an open meadow. I later learned that one of the last sightings of ivory-billed woodpeckers in the United State was made in this park, and the reclusive Florida panther has been sighted there as well.

From the park I took FL 634 on to Sebring, a small town of about 10,000 residents. Best known for the Sebring International Raceway, where the 12-hour Endurance Race is held each March, Sebring sits among rolling hills in south-central Florida. Orange groves extend for miles, interrupted occasionally by groves of towering palm and pine trees.

The town surrounds Lake Jackson, and much of the community's recreational activities take place on or near the lake.

With three public beaches, a number of public boat ramps, and a public pier for fishing, there is always plenty to do around the lake.

George Sebring, a ceramics manufacturer from Ohio, moved to the area in 1912 to create a new town in the wilderness. He selected a small oak tree to be its center, and all roads and streets of the town radiated out from a single road that circled a green where the tree stood. Businesses, many of which still exist, were built on the circle and a park was created inside it. This town plan was based on the pattern of the mythological Heliopolis (City of the Sun), with the park representing the sun, and the streets the rays radiating out from it.

I found the park and surrounding downtown area a pleasant place to walk and window-shop. The park and adjacent businesses were refurbished in the mid-1980s to look as they had in the 1920s. It is said that the pace of living was so slow in early Sebring that small children amused themselves by riding in carts pulled by large turtles. Life isn't that slow in the town now, but it is far from the madding pace found in the cities along the coast and around Orlando to the north.

You can return to Bradenton by the same route or you can spend the night at the Kenilworth Lodge on Lakeview Drive, just up the street from the downtown area. This restored landmark has a distinctive double-towered face that overlooks Lake Jackson across the street. Today the lodge is a 137-room bed-and-breakfast, and although I did not stay there, I was impressed by the lobby, with its grand fireplace blackened from years of use, and its winding staircase that leads up to guest rooms.

For More Information

De Soto National Monument (Bradenton): 813-792-0458

South Florida Museum (Bradenton): 813-746-4131

Gamble Plantation State Historic Site (Ellenton): 813-723-4536

Manatee Village Historical Park (Bradenton): 813-749-7165

Florida Cracker Trail Association (Bradenton):
    813-385-6136/5101 or 813-471-0001

Highlands Hammock State Park (Sebring): 941-386-6094

Sebring International Raceway (Sebring): 941-655-1442

Kenilworth Lodge (Sebring): 941-385-0111

11

Lake Okeechobee Loop

Getting there: From the town of Okeechobee take FL 441 south for three miles to the FL 441/78 junction. Turn right on FL 78 and continue around the west side of the lake for 34 miles to U.S. 27 at Moore Haven. Turn left on U.S. 27 and continue for 15 miles to Clewiston. Continue on U.S. 27 through Clewiston for 26 miles to South Bay and another two miles to County 715. Turn left and head north on County 715 another 15 miles to Pahokee. From Pahokee take U.S. 98/FL 441 around the east side of the lake 35 miles back to Okeechobee.

Highlights: Swampland Tours, Brighton Seminole Indian Reservation, Clewiston Inn, Pahokee State Park, Port Mayaca.

This trip begins at the small community of Okeechobee on the northern tip of Lake Okeechobee and soon enters an area of large cattle ranches. The first stop is at Swampland Tours, a birding and wildlife tour along the edge of Lake Okeechobee near the mouth of the Kissimmee River. This tour provides an excellent introduction to the ecology of the upper reaches of the Everglades and shows how large agricultural conglomerates have joined forces with the U.S. Army Corps of Engineers to alter the natural environment. Alligators, birds, turtles, and fish are all seen in abundance here, including such endangered species as the Everglades snail kite.

After the tour, the trip continues around the western shore of the lake for a short distance to County 721S. It heads north for 10 miles to the Brighton Seminole Indian Reservation, where you can drive through a peaceful and prosperous community with a thriving cattle business that provides the tribe with employment. From the reservation, return to FL 78 and continue through cattle and citrus country to the town of Moore Haven, where the Moore Haven Lock marks the beginning of the western portion of the Okeechobee Waterway.

U.S. 27 cuts through some of the largest stands of sugar cane in Florida, and takes you to the company town of Clewiston, where you can visit the Clewiston Inn and learn about the history of the U.S. Sugar Company. After a stop in Clewiston continue on U.S. 27 to South Bay, where you turn north to Pahokee and Pahokee State Park. Port Mayaca is the next stop, and there you can learn the story of the Okeechobee Waterway, which cuts across southern Florida from Port St. Lucie to Fort Myers. This waterway, the only navigable route across Florida from the Atlantic to the Gulf of Mexico, consists of the St. Lucie Canal, Lake Okeechobee, and the Caloosahatchee River.

Continue around the east side of the lake to the end of the route in Okeechobee.

This is a one- or two-day trip of 120 miles.

I thought I knew all about Lake Okeechobee, "The Big Waters," until I reached its shores just south of the town of Okeechobee. I knew that it was the largest freshwater lake in Florida and the second largest in the United States, and that it was the holding basin that fed the great river of grass to the south known as the Everglades. I also knew that the U.S. Army Corps of Engineers had spent years "developing" a flood control and water management system around the lake.

What I didn't know that really took me by surprise was that the entire 110-mile circumference of the lake is surrounded by a levee that averages almost 35 feet in height. It was a shock to drive up to the lake expecting to look out across a 730-square-mile surface and to discover instead that I couldn't even see the water.

Although I had a general idea of how all this dike work by the Corps of Engineers had affected the Everglades, I learned much more as I stopped to take a two-hour boat tour at the National Audubon Society Wildlife Sanctuary on Lake Okeechobee. The 28,500-acre sanctuary is located at the mouth of the Kissimmee River where it enters the lake, and it includes more than 10,000 acres of freshwater marsh that is rich in wildlife.

Barry "Chop" Lege, a third-generation Audubon guide from the Cajun country of southern Louisiana, leads the Swampland Tours and includes a history of the Okeechobee region in his tour narration. Until the 1950s the weather extremes of flood and drought controlled how and where people lived in south Florida, and the region around Lake Okeechobee, which is the geological head of the Everglades ecosystem, was lightly settled because of the vagaries of nature.

At that time Lake Okeechobee was simply a 730-square-mile shallow (the lake averages about 10 feet in depth) indentation where waters from the Upper Chain of Lakes that fed the Kissimmee River basin moved slowly over floodplains before emptying into the lake. In wet years the water continued to flow over the low southern rim of the lake into the upper reaches of the sawgrass marshes of the Everglades; in dry years it slowly filtered down into underground aquifers that then fed the lower marshes of the system. The overflow also fed the Caloosahatchee River to the west, and sometimes spread eastward as far as St. Lucie Inlet.

As population pressures increased in southern
Florida in the 1920s, more and more people moved
into the Lake Okeechobee region, and farmers
began to recognize the potential of the rich soil
found at the southern end of the lake. But nature
pays little heed to the safety of humans who
invade areas of extremes, and so something
had to give. And give it did, as several hurricanes hit the region in the late 1920s, killing
thousands as Lake Okeechobee overflowed its
banks in huge tidal waves that destroyed much of the
new development.

These disasters, as well as pressure from agricultural con-
cerns, led to the construction of the Herbert Hoover Dike
around the lake in 1930. The U.S. Army Corps of Engineers
also constructed a network of drainage canals, levees, stor-
age areas, and other flood control and water management
structures to allow large-scale agriculture development in the
area immediately south of the lake. While much applauded
during its construction, the project has come under increasing
attack by conservationists in recent years as we have gained a
better understanding of the needs of the Everglades ecosystem. Today the work of the Corps of Engineers is still sup-
ported by agricultural interests, as well as by most of the
residents of the Okeechobee region, but opposing forces have
curtailed the extent of the project to protect the real upper
reaches of the Everglades.

All of this was explained in detail by Barry Lege as he
pointed out the many natural residents of the region, such as
long-legged water birds and sunning turtles. Some of us came
away from the tour with a better understanding of the inter-
actions of the ecosystem, while others were still convinced
that the only real purpose of the vast reservoir was to slake
the thirst of the steadily increasing population of southern
Florida.

After listening to what had occurred around Okeechobee in the past half-century, I ventured about 10 miles down the road to the turnoff to the Brighton Seminole Indian Reservation, where I thought I might learn about what the region had been like before the intrusion of Europeans. I was disappointed in that search, but not with the reservation itself. The Brighton band of Seminoles there has developed a thriving cattle business, which has made the band almost indistinguishable from its surrounding neighbors. And it was refreshing to visit a reservation that flourishes economically.

That is not to say that the band has given up its Native American heritage. In fact, if you want to learn more about Seminole culture, you should plan to visit the reservation in February when it holds its annual Seminole Cultural Day in conjunction with the Brighton Field Days and Rodeo (held since 1938). Then you can watch great rodeo performers *and* get involved with Indian crafts, games, and storytelling events.

After driving around the reservation I returned to FL 78 and continued along the western shore of the lake, where big cattle ranches and scattered citrus groves are sparsely settled. By the time I reached the Moore Haven Lock and the beginning of the western section of the Okeechobee Waterway, the cattle ranches had given way to large stands of sugar cane. I passed by the lock without stopping and headed on to Clewiston.

Although no longer officially a company-owned town, there is no denying that Clewiston is a company town. From the time I first spotted the tall smokestacks and processing plants of the U.S. Sugar Company's plant until the moment I reached the company headquarters next door to the Clewiston Inn, I knew I was in a town ruled by Big Sugar.

The lobby of the whitewashed inn I entered looked like something right out of the 1930s or 1940s. In fact, it was built in 1938 by the young U.S. Sugar Corporation to house visiting company executives and other dignitaries. Clewiston Inn is the oldest hotel in the Lake Okeechobee area and claims to have been the center of all social activity in the upper Glades region since its construction. Whether this is true is debatable, since much of the social activity in the region would certainly be deemed unacceptable in the hallowed walls of the inn, where "society" meant only the upper crust.

This is apparent from the walls, paneled with bird's-eye cypress along the first-floor hallways, where photos extol the virtuous activities of former U.S. Sugar Company executives. These include photos of the company president presenting a check to local "Negro" leaders of the company-owned town of Harlem for the community's first swimming pool. This photo and others around recall, at least to me, a period in Southern history when the social structure rigidly defined racial and class differences that are no longer acceptable (at least on the surface). A side trip back up the highway to the small community showed me that Clewiston, and the U.S. Sugar Company, have not ventured far from the paternalistic attitudes of those earlier times. Harlem is still all black, poor, and controlled by the company, according to several local residents I talked with.

Instead of dining at the inn, I dedided to head on downtown, where I stopped at the funky Old South Bar-B-Q Ranch. This turned out to be one of the best—and least expensive—meals I have ever eaten in Florida. I sampled the pit barbecue dishes of pork, chicken, and beef, but settled on their all-you-can eat catfish plate.

The first platter was so large that I couldn't even finish it, although a customer at one of the neighboring tables not only finished his first plate, but had two others before complaining to the waitress that the food at the restaurant wasn't as good as it used to be. Oh well.

From Clewiston, I headed on around the southern end of the lake toward South Bay, and then turned north to Pahokee.

The Pahokee State Park campground and marina along the east shore of the lake is a fisherman's retreat, but there I learned about the Capt. JP Boat Cruises. These sightseeing and dinner cruises on a 400-passenger vessel operate between October and March and cruise on both Lake Okeechobee and the St. Lucie Canal. The cruises are two to four hours in length and go from Pahokee to Moore Haven and Stuart. I didn't take one because of time constraints, but they received high praise from departing passengers.

North from Pahokee I stopped at Port Mayaca Lock and Dam to watch several pleasure boats enter Lake Okeechobee from the St. Lucie Canal. This is only one of the five locks on the 152-mile length of the waterway, which is the only inland waterway across the Florida peninsula. You can gain a tour of these locks by asking Corps personnel, who will explain the locking process if they are not busy.

Between Port Mayaca and Okeechobee, the eastern shore of the lake becomes much more developed, with plenty of RV resorts and rental cabins for the thousands of fishermen who head to the lake for some of the best bass fishing in America. As I drove along this stretch, I thought that a good way to see the area would be to bike around the lake on top of the levee, but it was only after I got back into Okeechobee that I discovered that I was not the first person to think of this. One-hundred-ten miles of trail along the top of the dike have been designated as the Lake Okeechobee Scenic Trail, and this is a segment of the longer Florida National Scenic Trail, which runs the length of Florida. The longer scenic trail is one of only eight such trails in the nation, and no section is more easily accessible to everyone than the Okeechobee segment. With plenty of restaurants, stores, motels, campgrounds, and RV resorts scattered within easy access of the trail, hikers and bikers find the 110 miles easy to complete.

Although there is ready access at a number of locations around the lake, many people begin their travels at the trailhead, which is found at the Okee-Tantie Recreation Area where the Kissimmee River enters the lake.

Although this tour was much different than I expected, it gave me a much better understanding of some political realities concerning the attempt to save the Everglades—and it afforded some outstanding birding. Others will find the Southern hospitality, genteel living, and great fishing in the region more to their liking.

For More Information

Swampland Tours (Okeechobee): 941-467-9119

Brighton Field Days and Rodeo (Okeechobee): 941-763-7501

Clewiston Inn (Clewiston): 941-983-8151

Old South Bar-B-Q Ranch (Clewiston): 941-983-7756

Capt. JP Boat Cruises (Pahokee): 561-924-2100

Port Mayaca Lock (Port Mayaca): 561-924-2858

12

Fort Myers to Citrus Center to Pine Island

Getting there: From Fort Myers, follow FL 80 east for seven miles to FL 31. Follow FL 31 north to Babcock, then turn right on County 74 and head east for about 30 miles. Make a jog onto U.S. 27 south and continue south to County 78. Turn west on County 78 and continue through Citrus Center, La Belle, and Alva to Pine Island.

Highlights: Babcock Ranch, Cecil Webb Wildlife Management Area, Cypress Knee Museum, W. D. Franklin Lock and Dam, Museum of the Islands, Cayo Costa State Park.

The trip begins on FL 31 as it heads north through cattle-ranching country. The first stop is at Babcock Ranch. This working ranch includes thousands of acres of farm- and ranch land, and it also has a private game preserve where tourists can observe alligators, birds, and the elusive Florida panther from specially made swamp buggies.

After Babcock Ranch, tour the Cecil Webb Wildlife Management Area, and then follow a route that takes you through more ranching country to the Cypress Knee Museum. The return route follows the Caloosahatchee River and passes through La Belle and Alva before stopping by the W. D. Franklin Lock and Dam. The trip ends on Pine Island, the most northern of the bridged islands off Fort Myers.

This one-day trip is a 125-mile loop.

I hadn't planned to take this trip, and it was only from my wife's desire to have a cypress knee to replace a misplaced family heirloom that I did. I had gone to Fort Myers to begin the trip to Everglades City, and had told my wife that I would have no trouble finding some place in the region that sold polished knees. My search for such a business seemed destined to end in frustration, however, until one shop owner mentioned a cypress-knee museum not far from Lake Okeechobee.

Deciding to explore the area between Lake Okeechobee and Fort Myers a little as I searched for the museum, I headed north on FL 31. Commercial development ended abruptly as I entered Charlotte County to the north of Fort Myers, and broad expanses of pastureland became dominant. It soon became obvious that this was real cattle country, and large ranches that could have been part of Texas stretched for miles along both sides of the lightly traveled highway.

About 10 miles north of FL 80, I saw a sign for Babcock Ranch and Wilderness Adventures, and decided to find out what was there. For two miles, large fields of various crops lined both sides of the dirt road, and herds of cattle grazed in open pastureland. There was no doubt this was a working ranch, but where was the wilderness?

I found the beginning of it, at least, at the headquarters of the Crescent B Ranch. The Crescent B is a 153-square-mile ranch that the Babcock family has owned and operated since 1914. This property, the largest parcel owned by a single family in the southeastern United States, was acquired by lumber baron E. V. Babcock for its large stands of bald cypress, and he logged most of the cypress swamps on it during the 1930s. About 10,000 acres of trees were left in what is now called

Telegraph Swamp (named for the telegraph lines that had to be routed around it). Today this undisturbed tract of land is home to alligators, Florida panthers, and several hundred species of birds.

The original Babcock holdings were even larger, about 156,000 acres, but 65,000 acres were deeded to the state of Florida for the Cecil Webb Wildlife Management Area, which lies across FL 31 from the remaining ranch land. State officials were happy to acquire the land because it is such prime wildlife country, and they now use it as a protected panther habitat.

The abundance of wildlife in the backwaters of the ranch attracts thousands of Florida residents and tourists each year. The Babcock family leases most of the prime farm- and ranch land on their holdings to other farmers, but they maintain control over large tracts of wilderness and lead visitors on 90-minute tours through dark and primeval stretches of Telegraph Swamp. For these trips, guests are loaded onto large swamp buggies (converted from old trucks) that hold at least 30 passengers.

The tour leads through pastureland where you can see a bison herd, some unusual crossbreed cattle, and large herds of quarter horses; past open forest where you might see wild turkeys, feral pigs, deer, and other inhabitants of the open forest; and into the cypress swamps, where you will see water birds and alligators by the score. And you will never forget seeing the wild Florida panthers that roam the land here.

Although these are captive-bred animals contained within a large fenced area, they are wild in every other sense of the word. They have minimal human contact, and guests observe them behind unusual blinds that allow the animals to stay wild. The Babcocks have been so successful with their breeding program and with the release of their animals onto ranch property that the state fish-and-game department has expressed interest in acquiring even more of the ranch as a wildlife management site, including the panthers that are currently living there. For now, though, this is about the only place in Florida where you are almost guaranteed a chance to observe the reclusive panthers in the wild.

I found out when I visited the ranch that you must make tour reservations far in advance, and was unable to get a seat on one of the fascinating buggies. I did talk with several people who had just completed the tour, and all were very impressed with the quality and quantity of wildlife they had seen.

I also talked with several employees of the ranch who had lived in the area for their entire lifetimes, and heard stories about the wilder days when cattle and lumber barons engaged in wars and feuds matching any that had ever occurred in Texas. Tour leaders relate these colorful stories to guests as they pass by the old Cracker cowmen ranch houses.

Things are calm among the cattlefolk of the region now, but a constant battle between the large landholders and the state continues. The government is attempting to preserve more of the wilderness in parks and preserves, in an effort to increase the chances of survival for the panther and other endangered species of the region. The landowners have long been accustomed to ruling their fiefdom with minimal interference, and they aren't taking lightly the state's moves to acquire more land.

I backtracked to FL 31 and Tucker Grade Road on the west side of FL 31. I had learned about the Cecil Webb Wildlife Management Area while at Babcock Ranch, and wanted to explore it a little. I followed Tucker Grade Road a little over 10 miles west to the management area headquarters, where I gathered information about the activities there.

Hunting, fishing, and camping are the primary activities within the area. Much of the wildlife—such as red-cockaded woodpeckers, deer, coyotes, and armadillos—can be seen from Tucker Grade Road and two other roads, Oilwell Grade and Tram Grade, that lead into the interior of the area. These are to the north of Tucker Grade Road and do not lead back to FL 31, so I returned on Tucker Grade and then continued north on FL 31 for another six miles to Babcock Corner, where County 74 crosses FL 31.

I took a right on County 74 as it headed across more open land with large cattle spreads. I continued across this sparsely populated stretch for about 30 miles, to the end of County 74 near the junction of U.S. 27 and FL 29. I made the jog to U.S. 27 and headed south to what I thought would be a tourist stop at the Cypress Knee Museum. It was marked on the map, along with Gatorama, and I was sure that I would have no trouble finding it.

I did come to a small concrete-block building, where decaying and tilted letters proclaimed that it was the museum. I entered the parking lot, where grass grew high through the potholed asphalt, and found no one around. The building itself obviously had many cypress knees inside, but the door was locked and no signs revealed whether this was temporary or permanent. Thinking Gatorama might be more thriving, I headed down the road another two miles. The folks there directed me back toward the museum, but told me to look for a small house across the road. I slowed as I approached the museum, and, sure enough, there was a driveway leading to a rundown house with several outbuildings.

In a compound that looked like it was straight out of an isolated Appalachian valley, I found my wife a cypress knee. I was able to buy it, however, only after elderly owner Tom Gaskins's son helped me convince his father that I was worthy of owning one of his few remaining knees that weren't

true collector's items. The elder Gaskins had not collected
any new knees for several years because there had been a dis-
agreement between the owner of the nearby cypress groves
and the state about jurisdiction over the swamps where he
does his collecting.

After exploring the small museum and shop, which have
been located in these buildings since 1937, and walking along
a rickety boardwalk through a small swamp near Fisheating
Creek, I continued on my trip. I stayed on U.S. 27 (toward
Citrus Center) for about 10 miles past the museum as the
highway passed through rich farming country. At one time
this area had been the northern range of the Everglades, but
farmers in the earlier part of the century had drained the
swamps and turned the land into productive and rich farmland where vast orange groves now stand.

I turned west on County 78 at Citrus Center to head back to
Fort Myers, and found that the road paralleled the Caloosahatchee River, part of the only cross-Florida waterway, which
also includes the St. Lucie Canal and Lake Okeechobee. This
waterway, which is much like the never-completed cross-
Florida canal that had been planned on the St. Johns River
farther north, affords boats and barges an inland route from
St. Lucie Inlet on the Atlantic to Pine Island Sound on the
Gulf of Mexico.

The highway follows along the river through orange
groves to the junction of County 78 and FL 29 at La Belle.
This small town has a long history. The site of Fort Denaud
during the Second Seminole War in the early 1800s, the
remains of the fort can be found across the river from the
downtown. I didn't visit the fort, but was intrigued by the
large oak tree that stood beside the clock-towered courthouse. Local residents told me that it was one of the largest in
southwest Florida, which I found easy to believe. Its majestic
crown shaded a huge part of the courthouse square.

From La Belle I continued on County 78 as it headed west through farm country, and stopped at Alva to buy a pop at the century-old country store and museum. This fascinating little building tells many stories of early life in the region.

At the junction of County 78 and 78A between La Belle and Alva, I passed over the Turnstile Bridge. I later learned that this is one of the few bridges of this type, which is partially operated by hand, in Florida.

About 20 miles from La Belle I came to the W. D. Franklin Lock and Dam on the Caloosahatchee River. Part of the Okeechobee Waterway, this complex offers a picnic area, campground, and boat-launching ramp, as well as an overlook of the lock. I stopped to watch several boats go through the lock before I headed on to the end of the trip.

I had noted Pine Island on the map, and had decided to complete my day trip there. Having heard plenty about Sanibel and Captiva Islands, I expected Pine Island to be much like them. I was shocked as I drove over the bridge from Matlacha to the island itself to discover that there are no large condominiums or fancy shopping centers. And, as I was to find out, there are no long sandy beaches with excellent shells.

Pine Island is located in Pine Island Sound just north of Fort Myers, inside other barrier islands that include Sanibel, Captiva, North Captiva, Useppa, Cayo Costa, and Gasparilla. These outer islands capture the sand and shells as the gulf pushes toward the coast, and Pine Island is left protected from the constant pounding of the gulf waves. Consequently, it is unlike other barrier islands along the Gulf Coast. Instead of long beaches backed by low-lying dunes, Pine Island has lush plant growth, including thick stands of mangrove along the shore and large stands of loblolly pine inland. While Sanibel Island has been heavily developed in areas, Pine Island is still much as it was a century ago. Only about 7,000 people live on the 18-mile-long island, which was largely ignored by developers in the first half of this century. The island was not connected to the mainland by a bridge until 1927, and didn't receive electricity until 1941.

Today most island residents live in four communities: Matlacha, a commercial fishing village that sits on a small island near where a bridge connects Pine Island to the mainland and Cape Coral; Pineland, located on the west coast of the island, where residents can see the outer islands of Useppa and Upper Captiva in the distance; St. James City, located on the southern tip of Pine Island facing Sanibel Island across San Carlos Bay; and Bokeelia, located on the northern tip of the island, with some of the finest fishing piers in the world.

All of the small communities have a quiet charm that is far removed from the normal hustle and bustle of coastal Florida cities, but I saw some signs of encroachment from the rapid growth of Cape Coral. Luckily, island residents had the foresight to write and pass the Pine Island Ordinance some years ago, when high-rises were first planned for the island. This ordinance restricts building height to 38 feet, and keeps density low. In developed areas of the island there is a maximum of five units per acre, and in rural areas there is a limit of one unit per acre. I found the lack of resorts and RV parks refreshing, and spent several hours just walking around the fishing piers, talking to island residents and tourists who were enjoying some of the best fishing to be found in Florida.

In Bokeelia I visited the Museum of the Islands. This small museum opened in 1990 in the abandoned building of the original Pine Island Library. Although its collection activities are ongoing, there are a number of completed exhibits that tell of the island's early years. In the first room I learned about the early European settlements on the island, and in the second room I saw exhibits that explained more about the mounds that I had seen in Pineland. These were built by the Calusa Indians, who had lived on the islands for several thousand years before the invasion of the Spanish.

Be aware that while Pine Island is geographically close to the heavily traveled tourist sights near Fort Myers, it is in other ways so far removed from that world that it has almost no tourist facilities. If you don't like fishing and bird watching (the island is famous for the bald eagles that winter there), or you can't stand sitting on a veranda watching the sun set over the outer islands as it colors the calm waters of the gulf pink and then red, you won't like spending any time on Pine Island.

If you like the sound of these natural pleasures and would like to use Pine Island as a base from which to explore, you can arrange for boat trips to some of the outer islands. A particular favorite of many tourists is Cayo Costa, where Cayo Costa State Park is an excellent place to find shells. Shelling is best during the winter or after a storm.

Cabbage Key, the former retreat of mystery novelist Mary Roberts Rinehart, is another popular destination, and a restaurant there whose walls are papered with autographed dollar bills, offers excellent meals. On Cabbage Key you can have lunch or dinner or stay at the Cabbage Key Inn near the Intercoastal Waterway. There are also short, self-guided nature trails nearby that take you through several plant communities.

If those quiet activities appeal to you, contact the Pine Island Chamber of Commerce about accommodations on the island. This could be your "enchanted island."

For More Information

Babcock Ranch and Wilderness Adventures (Punta Gorda):
  813-338-6367

Cecil Webb Wildlife Management Area (Punta Gorda):
  813-644-9577

Cypress Knee Museum (Palmdale): 813-675-2951

Museum of the Islands (Bokeelia): 813-283-1525

Cayo Costa State Park (Cayo Costa): 941-964-0375

Cabbage Key Inn (Cabbage Key): 813-283-2278

Greater Pine Island Chamber of Commerce (Matlacha):
    813-283-0888

13

Fort Myers to Everglades City

Getting there: Begin in Fort Myers on FL 82. Head southeast on FL 82 to Immokalee. From Immokalee, head southwest on County 946, then east on FL 858 to FL 29. Turn south on FL 29 and continue through Sunniland and Copeland to Everglades City.

Highlights: Corkscrew Swamp Sanctuary, Sunniland Cafe, Big Cypress National Preserve, Fakahatchee Strand State Preserve, Ochopee Post Office (smallest in the United States), Smallwood's Store, Everglades National Park, the Ten Thousand Islands.

The first stop on this trip is the Corkscrew Swamp Sanctuary, an Audubon Society preserve where the endangered wood stork abounds. South of Immokalee, the road bisects the Big Cypress National Preserve, where the elusive and endangered Florida panther lives. Before you reach I-75 (Alligator Alley), stop at the Sunniland Cafe in Sunniland. The food may not be great, but you will enjoy the signs.

At Copeland, take a right on Janes Scenic Drive to head 20 miles into the Fakahatchee Strand State Preserve. In Ochopee, you can see the smallest post office in the United

States, as well as visit the headquarters of the Big Cypress National Preserve.

Continuing into Everglades City, you can visit Small-wood's Store in Chokoloskee and the western headquarters of the Everglades National Park, and take a boat tour of the western Everglades and the Ten Thousand Islands.

This full-day trip is about 130 miles one-way.

The previous route, Fort Myers to Citrus Center to Pine Island, took me through some of the Everglades land that had been drained for agricultural purposes early in this century, and the first portion of this did also. As I drove southeast along FL 82 from Fort Myers, I passed through some of the most productive watermelon-growing land in the country.

When I reached Immokalee I quickly left that tamed land for a section of wild Florida, as I followed County 846 16 miles to the south and west of Immokalee to the Cork-screw Swamp Sanctuary. This Audubon Society preserve, located in the northern portion of the Big Cypress Swamp, is the most-visited Audubon Sanctuary in the United States, but I walked in solitude along a self-guided, 1.75-mile boardwalk loop here during midweek in June. It's more crowded in the dry winter season between October and May.

This preserve has the largest stand of mature bald cypress in the country. Many of these trees are nearly 500 years old, and all provide shelter for a wide variety of flora and fauna. The forest was quiet as I strolled along, but if I had been there during wood stork nesting time (which can be any time between December and April), it would have reverberated with the raucous sounds of young hatchlings and mature adults as they frantically called for and served food.

The sanctuary is the nesting site of the largest colony of wood storks in the nation, but the number of storks nesting each year has dropped from thousands in the late 1950s to hundreds today, as massive drainage projects have drastically reduced the surface water supply both inside and outside the 11,000-acre preserve. Even the preserve itself was doomed to be drained in the early 1950s before local conservationists rescued it from development.

Since the water level within the preserve fluctuates about 4.5 feet during the year, what you can see as you walk through it varies by season. When I was there in June after a rainy spring, the area was lush and green, with few nesting birds. At any time you will see some of the more than 200 species of birds that have been identified there, with over 60 of those nesting in the foliage.

After a pleasant trek through Corkscrew Swamp, I returned to County 846, headed south, and took a left on FL 858 to FL 29. This stretch of road took me through an untamed section along the northern edge of the Big Cypress Swamp. Although the swamp appeared to me to be impenetrable and immune to development, that isn't so. Modern construction techniques make it possible for homes and cities to be built almost anywhere in southern Florida, and local conservationists are constantly at war with developers to keep large tracts of swamp wild.

At FL 29 I headed south. Just south of FL 858 on FL 29, I came to a sign in the small community of Sunniland that read "Sunniland Cafe—Terrible Food—Worse Service—Far Out Place—Far Out People—Welcome." I couldn't resist stopping, and encountered more such signs, such as "Welcome to Beautiful Downtown Sunniland. Home of the Famous Sunniland Country Club. Eat Here and Get Gas and Worms." The food was only passable but inexpensive. As the cafe owners say, "You've got to do something to attract people out here in the swamps."

And swamps there are. The Big Cypress National Preserve is named for its vastness, not the size of the cypress trees that grow there. Most of the cypress trees here are dwarf pond cypress, not the majestic bald cypress that I saw at Corkscrew Swamp. There is nothing small about the extent of the wilderness included in the 2,400-square-mile preserve, though, and it seemed as though I drove through it forever.

South of Sunniland signs began to pop up that indicated this was Florida panther country. In fact, all of the land south of Sunniland to Alligator Alley and to the west of FL 29 is the Florida Panther National Wildlife Refuge. Little is known about this secretive creature except that its numbers have decreased so much over the years that it is now endangered; the Florida panther lives in the wildlands of Big Cypress Swamp and the Everglades.

Because the dense, thickly vegetated swamps in Big Cypress tend to be long and narrow, locals have long called these areas *strands,* and Fakahatchee Strand, 20 miles long and three to five miles wide, is the largest in the region. Much of this swamp lies to the north of Alligator Alley and is privately owned. South of Alligator Alley the land to the west of FL 29 is protected as the Fakahatchee Strand State Preserve. Ecologically, this area is no different from that to the east of the road, which is protected as the Big Cypress National Preserve. It is just protected by a different governmental agency.

When I reached a wide spot in the road known as Copeland, I turned right on Janes Scenic Drive. I followed the road some 20 miles as it wound through wild swamplands full of alligators, waterbirds, and feral pigs. At the end of the 20 miles, when I reached the preserve boundary, I discovered why the creation of the preserve had been necessary. Although the condition of the road seemed to change for the better at the boundary, park maps recommend against traveling past that point. Maybe this recommendation is needed to keep people from seeing just what modern developers can do to this primeval region.

As I followed the road past the preserve boundary, I felt as though I had entered a holocaust zone. Paved and unpaved roads formed a grid that cut through what had been densely vegetated swamp, but which had long since been drained by arrow-straight canals. No houses stood on the lots along the deserted streets, for I had entered a failed real-estate development that now stood as a sad commentary on how to needlessly destroy almost a quarter-million acres of wild and wonderful swamp.

The area had been brutalized, but it is already showing signs of making a comeback. The canals have slowly filled, so that seasonal floodwaters cover the thousands of lots where homes were never built. Although it's too late to restore the natural beauty of the area, there is talk of setting aside this huge segment of the Big Cypress Swamp to help protect southern Florida's vanishing water supply. The roads and canals may be removed in an attempt to return the region to a more natural state, but there is no way to return this world to what it was before the land speculators made their attempt to civilize it.

Even with the roads and canals intact, the swamp is reclaiming the land for itself, and I was glad that I had taken the time to view this nightmarish sight. It strongly reinforced my already conservationist views about preserving the remaining wetlands of southern Florida.

I backtracked to FL 29 and continued to the junction of FL 29 and U.S. 41. There I took a short detour east on the Tamiami Trail (U.S. 41) to the headquarters of the Big Cypress National Preserve at Ochopee. Although the park headquarters did not have a visitors center (the preserve's visitors center is located about 20 miles farther east at the Oasis Visitor Center), it did have information about the region, and I obtained maps there that indicated roads and trails in the preserve that I could use on any further explorations of the region.

Ochopee Post Office

I also stopped to photograph what is reputed to be the smallest post office in the United States. This small building stands alongside U.S. 41 in Ochopee, and the flag that flies above it is almost large enough to cover one side of the building's roof.

I returned to FL 29; before heading five miles south to Everglades City, the western gateway to Everglades National Park, I stopped at the welcome station of the Everglades Area Chamber of Commerce, at the corner of FL 29 and U.S. 41. There I picked up brochures that told me what to do and see in the region.

Everglades City sits at the tip of mainland Florida. South of the city is the mangrove wilderness known as Florida's last frontier, the Ten Thousand Islands region. This area is a dream come true for naturalists and fishermen. In canoes and boats, tourists can travel along well-marked routes into this island maze in search of dolphins, pelicans, eagles, alligators, and manatees.

Before investigating any of the many boat rides and tours that are advertised along the waterfront in Everglades City, I drove through town and continued all the way to Smallwood's Store in Chokoloskee. This wood-frame building, which stands on stilts above the gulf waters, is one of the oldest buildings in southwest Florida.

The historic store, which was established in 1906 and has been on the National Register of Historic Places since 1974, now houses a museum and gift shop instead of the multitude of supplies that it once stocked. At one time it was the only grocery, hardware, and dry goods store for the many settlers and Seminole Indians who lived among the isolated islands and hammocks of the Ten Thousand Islands and the western Everglades.

Peter Matthiessen based his bestseller *Killing Mister Watson* on an event that occurred outside the store in 1910. A group of locals shot Ed Watson, a leader of one of the largest pioneer families in the area, after questioning him about several employees who had disappeared before they could collect their pay.

Chokoloskee is the jumping-off point for many fishing expeditions in the Ten Thousand Islands region, and has several marinas with fishing guides who help tourists gain access to this fishing wonderland.

After visiting Smallwood's Store I returned to Everglades City, where I enjoyed the Everglades National Park Gulf Coast Visitor Center. There I learned about the narrated boat tours that take visitors into the mangrove swamps and estuaries common to the region. Before I went on one of these tours, however, I wandered about the exhibits at the visitors center, which explain how this large "river of grass" that is called the Everglades really is a river, but a very unusual one. While the Big Cypress area is a great depression, where swamps are broken up by the high ground of hardwood hammocks, pine flatlands, and open, dry prairies, the Everglades area is an extremely large river.

Some ten thousand years ago, only the blink an an eye in geological time, all of southern Florida was covered by a shallow sea much like what Florida Bay is now. This sea covered the foothills of the Appalachian Mountains, and, over millions of years, compressed the shells and skeletons of various sea animals into a flat layer of limestone.

The peat soil that has developed over this layer of limestone since the seas receded is very thin, and few plants can thrive in it. With the flat terrain and poor growing conditions, the Everglades River developed—more than 100 miles long, 50 miles wide, and only inches deep much of the year. The water for this river comes from the seasonal overflow of Lake Okeechobee, the catch basin of the Kissimmee River drainage system. The wide, shallow Everglades River has a slope of only inches per mile, so its current is almost imperceptible, but this slow movement of shallow water has allowed the rich ecosystem of the Everglades to develop.

This river once covered all of southern Florida, from Lake Okeechobee to the Gulf of Mexico, but during the first half of this century, humans began to manipulate the ecosystem. Canals were built to drain land for agriculture; flood-protection projects were designed after a devastating hurricane around Lake Okeechobee resulted in tremendous loss of life; and water projects were built to supply the ever-growing needs of expanding cities along the Atlantic coast (see Chapter 11). All of these projects diverted water from the lower Everglades as the upper portion disappeared. The Everglades National Park now includes less than 10 percent of the original Everglades, and less than 50 percent of the original area is even marginally intact.

It hardly seems possible that the wilderness area could have been so much larger, however, or that any significant amount of water had been diverted from the region, sitting aboard one of the tour boats operated as a national park concession. The mangrove swamps seemed never-ending, and there certainly is no lack of water where we were cruising. We saw abundant wildlife, including herons, egrets, eagles, dolphins, and alligators. All of this was somewhat illusory, though, for such degradation took place during the first part of the century (and is still occurring) that the Everglades ecosystem is seriously threatened.

Back on land, I wandered around Everglades City and found a delightful, funky eating place. The Rod and Gun Club, established in the 1920s as a hunting and fishing lodge, attracted the famous and not-so-famous for decades. These guests came to enjoy the bountiful fishing in the region and to savor the fruits of their efforts after they were cooked in the kitchen at the luxurious lodge. William S. Allen, the first permanent white settler in the region, built the lodge in 1883 as his home. Barron Collier later converted the large home to the Rod and Gun Club.

Collier attracted actors, writers, royalty, and four U.S. presidents to his club. In 1958 Burl Ives and Gypsy Rose Lee stayed there during the filming of *Winds Across the Everglades*. The lodge was severely damaged by Hurricane Donna in 1960, and after a period of hard times, a fire destroyed the motel section of the resort in 1973. Some cottages still survive, as does a screened-in, heated swimming pool. The captivating parts of the lodge that have survived are the magnificent old lobby with cypress walls covered by trophy-size fish, and the huge, dark, cypress-paneled dining hall in which both food and service are still good. I had my meal of frog legs outside (on the screened porch), where I could watch small boats come and go, and imagined myself sitting among the famous guests of yore.

The one thing I didn't get to do on this trip is almost as important as all that I did. The 110-mile Wilderness Waterway begins near Everglades City, then winds through the western edge of the Everglades National Park and the Ten Thousand Islands before it ends at the Flamingo Visitor Center at the southern tip of the park. This well-marked trail has several backcountry campsites that are spaced about a day's canoeing apart.

Canoeing on the quiet waters of Florida is a favorite activity of mine, and the next time I visit Everglades City, it will be to take a weeklong canoe trip along this trail.

Return to Fort Myers on U.S. 41 or spend the night at one of the cottages of the Rod and Gun Club.

For More Information

Corkscrew Swamp Sanctuary (Naples): 941-657-3771

Sunniland Cafe (Sunniland): 941-657-6661

Big Cypress National Preserve (Ochopee): 941-695-4111

Fakahatchee Strand State Preserve (Copeland): 941-695-4593

Everglades Area Chamber of Commerce (Everglades City): 941-695-3941

Smallwood's Store (Chokoloskee): 941-695-2989

Everglades National Park (Everglades City): 941-695-3311

Everglades National Park Boat Tours (Everglades City): 941-695-2591 or 800-445-7724

Rod and Gun Club (Everglades City): 941-695-2101

14

Florida City to Key West

Getting there: From Miami, take U.S. 1 south to Florida City, the starting point for this trip. Follow U.S. 1 south to Key West, then reverse the route to return to Florida City.

Highlights: Bicycle tour, Half Shell Raw Bar & Fish Market, Turtle Kraals, Key West Lighthouse, Bat Tower, National Key Deer Refuge, Bahia Honda State Park, Museum of Natural History of the Florida Keys, Dolphin Research Center, John Pennekamp Coral Reef State Park.

Virtually my first stop on this route was at the end of the road, in Key West. There I visited Mallory Square; took a bicycle tour; saw the Key West Lighthouse, the southernmost point in the continental United States; and walked around the City of Key West Cemetery.

On the return trip I stopped at the Bat Tower, the National Key Deer Refuge, and Bahia Honda State Park in the Lower Keys. In the Upper Keys I visited the Museum of Natural History of the Florida Keys, the Dolphin Research Center, and the John Pennekamp Coral Reef State Park.

This two-day journey is about 250 miles round-trip.

I had last visited the Florida Keys in 1960, and had memories of small fishing villages with laid-back residents who had little interest in the tourists who were invading their area. In those days the Overseas Highway, often called the Highway to the Sea, was a narrow, two-lane road that became a 130-mile traffic jam on busy holiday weekends but was lightly traveled during midweek and off-season.

The keys are a group of some 800 coral islands that extend along the only coral reef in North America, from Miami on the east coast of Florida southwest into the Gulf of Mexico. Since I knew that I would have to return along the Overseas Highway after visiting Key West, I decided to pick up information at various visitors centers, but to linger on the way to Key West only when something truly struck my fancy. I would then stop at most sites on the way back to Miami.

From Florida City in the north to Key West in the south, small green signs with white numerals stand alongside U.S. 1. These mark the miles you have traveled along the Overseas Highway. They begin with Mile Marker 126, just south of Florida City, and end with Mile Marker 0 in Key West. These markers make it easy to give directions in the keys, and most residents use them when telling you how to reach any given spot.

The Overseas Highway generally follows the route of Henry Flagler's Florida East Coast Railroad, which extended from Jacksonville in the north to Key West in the south. Rail workers endured seven years of hazards and hardships to construct the 130 miles of rail and trestles between Florida City and Key West before Key West was connected to the mainland by rail in 1912. Trains traversed the route for only 23 years before the Labor Day Hurricane in 1935 destroyed the railway and wiped out dozens of the 42 train trestles that connected the various keys. In 1938, the railway was replaced by the Overseas Highway, which used the railroad right-of-way and remaining trestles; the route has been upgraded several times since then.

As I crossed over Blackwater Sound to Key Largo on this trip, I could see things had changed. The highway had been widened, and tourist stops dominated both sides of the road where I stopped at the Key Largo Chamber of Commerce and Florida Visitors Center at Mile Marker 106. I found the road and bridges much wider than I had remembered, and the drive through the keys was a pleasant one as I gazed out over the contrasting waters of the Atlantic on the left and the gulf on the right. I continued all the way to Key West without another stop, for I wanted to get to Mallory Square in time for sunset, which I had remembered as a festive occasion.

All along the way I saw signs of tourism that had not been apparent some 30 years earlier. Hotels and condominiums now rise above mangrove swamps, and what were once sleepy fishing villages are now thriving tourist resorts. As I passed from the Upper Keys and crossed over the new Seven-Mile Bridge, this heavy development decreased somewhat. The 65-foot-high structure, which opened in 1982 and is probably the most photographed bridge in the world after the Golden Gate, adds an extra dimension to the drive. Nowhere else on the Keys can you gain such a panoramic view of the open water and the Lower Keys; the blue waters reach the horizon on both the east and the west. The original wood-and-concrete structure still stands beside the new bridge but is closed to automobiles. Pedestrians and cyclists use it, however, and it is often called the world's longest fishing pier.

I reached the end of the road in Key West, the southernmost city in the United States, and found that the decrease in development I had noticed in the Lower Keys after I passed over the Seven-Mile Bridge did not carry over into Key West. There is little open space left on the last large key in the chain, and Key West seemed to be one large tourist site as I made my way through town to Jabour's Trailer Court, near Old Town and the waterfront. I was driving a pickup truck with cab-over camper, and wanted to get it parked so I could make my way around downtown without having to worry about navigating through narrow streets. While I didn't stay in one of the popular bed-and-breakfasts that abound in the city, you may want to check out one of them. Eden House and the Popular House, for example, both look interesting.

Many first-time visitors to Key West catch the Conch Tour Train or the Old Town Trolley for hour-and-a-half tours of the more popular sightseeing sections of Key West, but I chose a less traditional option. I stopped by the Old Town Bicycle Rental just a few blocks from Jabour's, rented a bicycle, and met a Key West Nature Bike Tour group at the Moped Hospital on the corner of Truman and Simonton. From there we took an hour-and-a-half ride around the city, during which we learned about the flora of the keys. In addition, we saw many of the usual historical sights, such as the Audubon House and Gardens, Hemingway House, Truman's Little White House, and the Donkey Milk House.

This was the perfect way to take a quick tour of this small island, which measures barely four miles long and two miles wide, as well as get in a little exercise after a day's drive. After returning my bicycle to the rental place, I walked to the docks at Mallory Square to enjoy one of nature's great treats—and one of Key West's few free tourist attractions.

Sunset is a big event in the Keys, and in the past decade or so has become a major attraction in Key West. People begin gathering at Mallory Square hours before sunset to wait for the colorful show as the sun drops below the horizon over the gulf, and on those days when clouds form a reflective screen for the sinking sun, the western sky and gulf waters turn into a kaleidoscope of reds, pinks, and oranges.

This natural attraction has become so popular that dozens of street artists and sellers now collect in Mallory Square to hawk their wares to the large crowds that collect to watch the sunsets. One of these is the now-famous Cookie Lady. In the early 1980s the Cookie Lady, who goes by no other name, began appearing at Mallory Square just before sunset to sell homemade cookies from a large box on the back of her bicycle. She lets customers pay what they wish for cookies or brownies as she dispenses poems to all within hearing distance. She will even create spontaneous ditties that play on first names or hometowns as she peddles among the crowd.

The Cookie Lady is only one of dozens of town characters I saw in experiencing my first Key West sunset in more than 30 years. While the number of people who congregated at Mallory Square had increased tremendously over those years and the square had taken on a carnival-like atmosphere instead of a quiet, contemplative one, the quality of the sunsets had not diminished in the least.

After sunset I walked around Old Town, wandering into art shops that sold high-quality local art, and I stood next to tourist traps that sold the same shoddy goods found in tourist spots all over America. Old Town offers something to suit just about every taste, and that includes at least a hundred of the best seafood restaurants in the nation.

I found my favorite at Land's End Village. There the Half Shell Raw Bar & Fish Market sits next to the Turtle Kraals, a reminder of the times when early settlers kept giant sea turtles, an important source of food to them, in pens near the docks. Today the turtles are protected, and those that are kept in the pens are part of a free exhibit that I enjoyed on my after-dinner walk. There is also a restaurant and bar at the Kraals, but I chose to eat at the Half Shell.

The Half Shell Raw Bar sits on the marina, where the scenery included sun-pinked clouds left over from an afternoon storm and hovering just above the distant horizon. The restaurant itself is very informal, with varnished picnic tables and a chalkboard menu; the food is excellent.

Although Key West is the last inhabited island in the Florida Keys, the Dry Tortuga Islands, which are located in the

Gulf of Mexico about 70 miles *west* of Key West, are also part of the chain. Thomas Jefferson once planned a fort for the Dry Tortugas, which get their name from the fact that there is no fresh water on them, but construction did not begin on it until 1846.

The fort was never completed, due to construction problems. Although it never saw military action, it was used as a federal prison for a time, and Dr. Samuel Mudd, who set John Wilkes Booth's leg after the assassination of Abraham Lincoln, was incarcerated there for some time. I didn't visit Fort Jefferson, which is maintained by the National Park Service, but was told time and again that I should take the half-day seaplane flight to the islands. The low-flying planes supposedly give you the most spectacular views available of the Florida Keys. Maybe next time.

Before heading back to Miami, I did visit the southernmost point in the continental United States, the Key West Lighthouse, which is closer to Havana than Miami, and the City of Key West Cemetery.

The base of the present lighthouse was built on Whitehead Street in 1848; another 20 feet had to be added to the tower in 1894 to make it more visible to seagoing ships. Keepers manned the tower for some 120 years before the Coast Guard closed it in 1969. It was opened for public tours in 1972, and was completely restored between 1987 and 1990.

I was only one of thousands of tourists who climb the tower each year to view Key West and the surrounding waters. The 88 steps that lead to the watchroom try the physical endurance of some, but the view is unsurpassed in the southern Keys.

The cemetery has a number of interesting headstones and mausoleums, such as that of B. P. Roberts, who died June 18, 1979. A plaque on the Roberts family mausoleum reads, "I told you I was sick." The cemetery is also one of the best

Key West Lighthouse

birding sites in Key West. There is little open space on the island, and birds use the cemetery as a stopover point during migration periods.

After looking around the cemetery, where the plots have been recycled so many times that some graves hold the bones of dozens of burials, I returned to the Overseas Highway for the return trip. I used this portion of the journey to stop at some of the interesting sites that I had learned about on my way to Key West.

The first of these was the Bat Tower on Sugarloaf Key. This unusual, louvered bat condominium was built in 1929 by Righter C. Perky to protect his fishing-camp guests from the hoards of mosquitoes that rose from the surrounding swamps. His thought was to build the tower, import bat guano from Texas, and attract bats with the smell. Unfortunately, the smell drove away the guests and didn't attract any bats. To reach the tower, turn left at Mile Marker 17.

My next stop was more interesting, for it was at the National Key Deer Refuge Headquarters on Big Pine Key. Key deer are the smallest subspecies of the Virginia white-tailed deer, and grow only to about the size of a large dog. Their fawns weigh only two to four pounds at birth, and adults reach 24 to 28 inches in height.

Only about 300 of these deer are left on the Keys, and 60 to 70 are killed each year in traffic accidents. Because of this loss, speed limits are strictly enforced on Big Pine Key. I learned about the refuge at the headquarters and visitors center before taking the nature trail to an old limestone quarry in the middle of the refuge at Watson's Hammock. I didn't see any deer on my walk (they are most often seen in the early morning and at dusk), but I did see several large alligators in the fresh water of Blue Hole, as the pond in the old quarry is called. This pond is the largest body of fresh water in the Keys.

The best times to visit the refuge are between April and June, when the fawns are born, and between August and early September, when the bucks leave traces of antler velvet on trees and brush during rutting season. You reach the refuge by turning west at Mile Marker 30.5 on Big Pine Key.

At Mile Marker 37 I left the Overseas Highway to enter the Bahia Honda State Park. One of the best beaches in the Keys, and in all the nation according to one recent survey, is found in this park, which is the southernmost state park in Florida. I only strolled along the beach, but the swimming here is said to be excellent. I saw several rare plants on the nature trail, and the bird life was abundant.

I continued north from Bahia Honda and returned to the heavily developed Upper Keys after crossing the Seven-Mile Bridge. I passed through Marathon, which is one of the most developed towns in the Keys, and continued until I reached the Museum of Natural History of the Florida Keys at Mile Marker 50.

This new museum, which opened on Earth Day, 1991, contains excellent exhibits. It also has a nature trail that leads through a rare tropical-palm hammock. These hammocks are the only tropical forests found in the United States, and contain such plants as the poisonwood tree (a relative of poison sumac and poison oak) and the gumbo limbo tree, which is related to the types of trees that bear frankincense and myrrh.

After a short stay at the museum, I continued to Grassy Key. There I stopped at the Dolphin Research Center, which is marked by a gigantic dolphin sculpture in front. I got to pet some dolphins, and could have swum with them if I had so chosen. The dolphins, which are kept in a saltwater lagoon, are all refugees from theme parks, where they have become overstressed from years of performing.

My next stop was at Indian Key Fill, between Upper and Lower Matecumbe Keys at Mile Marker 78, where I just missed the last boat to Lignumvitae Key State Botanical Site. These three-hour trips take visitors to a 280-acre key covered with a virgin tropical forest. Rangers lead walks through this rare environment, which is a reminder of how the keys appeared before the Europeans arrived. I was disappointed, but I had dallied so long at previous stops that I had literally missed the boat. You can avoid this by calling ahead for times and reservations.

It was getting late in the afternoon, and I was only a little over halfway along the Overseas Highway, so I drove at a faster pace through Islamorada, which is just a large tourist stop to my eyes, to the restored village of Tavernier on Plantation Key. While one story has it that the name came from the fact that "there was always a tavern near," it is more likely that the village was named after a French pirate who plied his craft in the region.

Today this quiet village is a delightful stop. I walked around the historic area, which has more than 50 buildings with the white-plank siding and tin roofs typical of island architecture. I also stopped at the research station of the National Audubon Society. This station is found by turning east at Mile Marker 89. It is located in the second house on the left after you leave the Overseas Highway. I found this the best source on birding in the Keys, and picked up a lot of informative pamphlets while I was there.

My last stop was on Key Largo, at the John Pennekamp Coral Reef State Park. This was the first underwater park established in the United States, and I found it to be the most crowded and overused of all the parks and trails I visited in the Keys. (This is due to its proximity to Miami.) Many people stop their tour of the Keys here, never venturing any farther south.

Most people at the park seem to favor the glass-bottomed boats that explore the reefs about five miles offshore, but I rented a canoe to float around the edges of the mangrove forests, where I saw hundreds of birds. This was my last stop on this return to the Keys, and I found that much of my visit lacked the rural feeling the other routes in this guide offered. While the rest of the routes I chose for this guide had truly taken me along country roads, the Overseas Highway has long since turned into a popular tourist road along which the old Florida has been swept away by development. True, there are areas along the route where development has been minimal—the upper part of the Lower Keys, for example—but these are fewer than I had expected from my previous visits to the area.

Even with this dramatic increase in tourism, however, I still recommend this route as a "Don't miss." There is just too much history of old Florida in the Keys, and nowhere else in the continental United States can you find a true tropical paradise.

When I reached FL 905, just past Mile Marker 105 as I was leaving Key Largo, I decided to follow it to Card Sound Road. I was glad I did, for the toll bridge over the sound rises high above the Keys and provides a panoramic view of the southern edge of the Everglades. Cypress tree islands, mangrove forests, and open blue water extend nearly to the horizon, as the mainland hovers, barely visible, in the distance.

As I left this last route to return to Miami and urban Florida, I had nothing but good memories of my trips along rural Florida's country roads. You, too, can have these experiences any time you visit the state, for nowhere in Florida are you far from a country road that takes you away from the glitz and crowds of Florida's theme parks and sprawling cities.

For More Information

Jabour's Trailer Court (Key West): 305-294-5723

Eden House (Key West): 305-296-6868 or 800-533-KEYS

The Popular House (Key West): 305-296-7274

Conch Tour Train (Key West): 305-294-5161

Old Town Trolley (Key West): 305-296-6688

Old Town Bicycle Rental (Key West): 305-294-5723

Key West Nature Bike Tour (Key West): 305-294-1882

Audubon House and Gardens (Key West):
  305-294-2116

Hemingway House (Key West): 305-294-1575

Truman's Little White House (Key West): 305-294-9911

The Donkey Milk House (Key West): 305-296-1866

Half Shell Raw Bar & Fish Market (Key West):
  305-294-5028

Turtle Kraals (Key West): 305-294-5028

Fort Jefferson National Monument (Key West):
  305-247-6211

Key West Lighthouse (Key West): 305-294-0012

National Key Deer Refuge (Big Pine Key):
  305-872-2239

Bahia Honda State Park (Big Pine Key): 305-872-3897

Museum of Natural History of the Florida Keys (Marathon):
  305-743-9100

Dolphin Research Center (Marathon Shores):
305-289-0002

Lignumvitae Key State Botanical Site (Islamorada):
305-664-4815

John Pennekamp Coral Reef State Park (Key Largo):
305-451-1202

Index